Please return/renew this item by the last date shown
Thank you for using your library

Penguin Study Notes

WILLIAM SHAKESPEARE

Romeo and Juliet

SUSAN QUILLIAM, M.A.
Advisory Editor: STEPHEN COOTE, M.A., PH.D.

PENGUIN BOOKS

PENGUIN BOOKS

Published by the Penguin Group
Penguin Books Ltd, 27 Wrights Lane, London w8 5tz, England
Penguin Putnam Inc., 375 Hudson Street, New York, New York 10014, USA
Penguin Books Australia Ltd, Ringwood, Victoria, Australia
Penguin Books Canada Ltd, 10 Alcorn Avenue, Toronto, Ontario, Canada m4v 3b2
Penguin Books (NZ) Ltd, Private Bag 102902, NSMC, Auckland, New Zealand

Penguin Books Ltd, Registered Offices: Harmondsworth, Middlesex, England

First published in Penguin Passnotes 1985
Published in Penguin Study Notes 1999
10 9 8 7 6 5 4 3 2 1

Copyright © Susan Quilliam, 1985
All rights reserved

Set in 10/12.5 pt PostScript Monotype Ehrhardt
Typeset by Rowland Phototypesetting Ltd, Bury St Edmunds, Suffolk
Printed in England by Clays Ltd, St Ives plc

Contents

To the Student

This book is designed to help you with your studies and examinations. It contains an introduction to the play, analyses of scenes and characters, and a commentary on some of the themes and issues raised by the play. Line references are to the New Penguin Shakespeare edition, edited by T. J. B. Spencer (Penguin Books, 1967).

When you use this book, remember that it is no more than an aid to your study. It will help you to find passages quickly and perhaps give you some ideas for essays. But remember: *This book is not a substitute for reading the play, and it is your response and knowledge that matter.* These are the things the examiners are looking for, and they are also the things that will give you the most pleasure. Show your knowledge and appreciation to the examiner, and show them clearly.

Introduction

The tragedy of *Romeo and Juliet* is one of the most famous love stories of all time. It was known and told as prose, poetry and drama many times before Shakespeare wrote his play, and there have been many versions since. These now include film, television and radio presentations.

The reasons for the success of the basic story are that it spans so many of the essential elements in human life – falling in love, conflict, death; it includes many characters with whom we can identify – the young lovers, the helpful Nurse, the villain, the dominant father; it raises our basic human emotions – laughter, fear, joy, anger, sorrow.

Shakespeare's working of the story makes a masterpiece from an already successful basis. We become deeply involved in what is happening, not only because of the way in which the plot is presented, the story telescoped, one event leading inexorably on to the next, but also because of the skilful development of characters and because Shakespeare has used the story to present us with complex insights into the nature of love, conflict, death and fate.

The plot is one of constant action, erupting on to the stage with an exciting fight, then straight away involving us in the plight of the lovers and how they are drawn together. The scene where Romeo first meets Juliet is delicately and sensitively handled, as is the balcony scene where they exchange love vows. Almost immediately they are married, and thereafter the love story turns into a tragedy which we – but not the lovers – know cannot be stopped. The dramatic fight in the middle of the play leads inexorably to Romeo's act of revenge and his banishment. The intended marriage to Paris leads to Juliet's horrific drinking of the potion, and one mishap after another leads to the final act of the tragedy. The climax, the double suicide, stirs emotion in a way that few other dramatic endings can.

The characters presented here also add to our involvement in the play. The young, innocent lovers raise our sympathy for their youth and their tragic end. Tybalt, the villain, is a constant threat. The support of the Nurse and the Friar is a source of comfort – until it goes wrong. Juliet's parents stir our resentment, and we love the bright energy of Mercutio, feeling his loss as Romeo does.

Both plot and characters are unified by the fact that, throughout, Shakespeare presents similar and contrasting viewpoints on a number of themes. We see many different aspects of love: romantic, bawdy, maternal, material. We see conflict examined through the family feud, the conflict of generations, the personal conflict between individuals. We see, as a result of all these forms of conflict, the ever-present reality of death. And over everything we see the supposed influence of fate, and we examine how far, in fact, it does affect events.

And, of course, all these elements – the plot, the people involved and the themes examined – are presented by Shakespeare in a form that increases the effect of the drama on us. Shakespeare's language and verse are used skilfully to create a wide range of ideas and emotions in us, to raise images in our minds that greatly enhance the effect of what is happening on stage.

It is possible, then, to react to *Romeo and Juliet* on many different levels, as a simple love-story about two young people, and as complex and beautifully worked tragedy.

Synopsis of Romeo and Juliet

The Chorus introduces the play, welcomes us and outlines the tragic story of the two lovers whose deaths unite their feuding families (The Prologue).

The play opens with a brawl between the Capulets and the Montagues, two families of Verona. The fight is stopped by the Prince of Verona, Escalus, who berates both sides for their continuing feud and threatens death to anyone who commits violence again. Lord and Lady Montague are concerned for their son, Romeo, who appears depressed. Benvolio, their nephew, offers to help. When he speaks to Romeo, the lad admits that he is suffering from unrequited love (I, i).

Meanwhile, the Capulets are attempting to arrange a marriage for their daughter to a young nobleman, Paris. Lord Capulet suggests that Paris conducts his suit at the Capulet feast that night. Romeo and Benvolio happen to see the guest list for the feast. Realizing that Romeo's beloved, Rosaline, is to be there, Benevolio suggests that they too attend so that Romeo may recover from his infatuation by comparing Rosaline with fairer beauties (I, ii).

In the Capulet household, Juliet's mother tells the girl of Paris's interest in her and, encouraged by her old Nurse, Juliet innocently agrees to accept his courtship (I, iii).

On the way to gatecrash the Capulet feast, Romeo and his friends joke and bandy words. Mercutio, a relative of the Prince, and an intelligent but mercurial man, is in particularly high spirits. Romeo, however, is filled with a strange sense of foreboding (I, iv).

Romeo enters the feast, and almost immediately sees Juliet and falls passionately in love with her. The attraction is mutual, and the two meet, exchange words and kiss. Romeo's presence at the ball, however, is noticed by Juliet's cousin, the aggressive Tybalt. Tybalt wishes to kill Romeo there and then, but is prevented by Lord Capulet, who tries to keep the peace. Further hints of future danger come as both Romeo and Juliet discover that they are members of opposing families (I, v).

Act II is once again opened by the Chorus, commenting on Romeo's new-found but dangerous love.

Romeo himself, having left the Capulet house at the end of the feast, cannot leave Juliet. Though his friends Mercutio and Benvolio are trying to find him, he gives them the slip. After exchanging bawdy jokes about Romeo's infatuation with Rosaline, the two young men go home (II, i).

Meanwhile, Romeo has climbed over a wall into the Capulet garden, and there sees Juliet on the balcony. For a while he watches her, then steps forward, and the lovers greet each other, at first warily, then with more and more open declarations of love. When Juliet suggests that they marry, Romeo agrees enthusiastically and says he will meet her messenger the following morning to inform her of the arrangements. After prolonged farewells, the lovers part (II, ii).

Romeo goes to confide in his confessor, Friar Laurence, a simple but well-meaning monk. After expressing concern that Romeo has changed his attention so swiftly from Rosaline to Juliet, the Friar agrees to marry the lovers, hoping that this marriage will help to end the family feud (II, iii).

The next morning, Mercutio and Benvolio are wondering where Romeo was the previous night; they are also concerned that Tybalt has now issued a challenge to Romeo. Romeo appears, back to his happy, witty self, and after joking with his friends, meets Juliet's Nurse. They arrange that Juliet shall go to Friar Laurence's cell that afternoon for the wedding ceremony and that Romeo shall come to Juliet's room that night to consummate the marriage (II, iv).

Juliet is anxiously waiting for news. When the Nurse returns, she teases Juliet by refusing to say what has happened, but eventually tells her of the wedding arrangements, and the girl happily goes off to Friar Laurence's cell (II, v).

At the cell, Friar Laurence waits to perform the ceremony, warning

Romeo of the dangers of hasty love. When Juliet arrives, the Friar leads the lovers off to be married (II, vi).

Act III opens later that afternoon. Mercutio and Benvolio are accosted by Tybalt, who wishes to fight a duel with their friend Romeo. When Romeo himself appears, straight from his secret marriage, he meets Tybalt's insults with courtesy. Mercutio, outraged by Romeo's apparent submission, answers the Capulet challenge himself. Romeo tries to part the duellists, and Mercutio is fatally wounded under Romeo's arm.

Enraged by the death of his friend, seemingly brought about by his own love-caused weakness, Romeo turns on Tybalt and kills him. He flees and is banished in his absence by Prince Escalus (III, i).

Juliet, meanwhile, is impatiently waiting for Romeo to come to her. The Nurse appears with the tragic news, but after her first emotional outburst against Romeo Juliet thinks the situation through and finds herself even more deeply in love with her husband (III, ii).

Romeo, in hiding with Friar Laurence, is, however, violently depressed. Even when he hears that the expected sentence of death for his crime has been commuted to banishment, he is so terrified by the outcome of his actions that he tries to commit suicide. The Friar convinces him of the possibility of a good outcome, and Romeo agrees to continue with his plan of spending the night with Juliet, then accepting banishment in Mantua until everything is reconciled (III, iii).

Unfortunately, Juliet's parents are in the meantime proceeding with their arrangements for her marriage to Paris (III, iv).

After spending the night together, the lovers are unwilling to part, but Romeo eventually leaves for Mantua. Juliet recovers herself enough to face her mother, who has come with news of her impending marriage to Paris. Juliet angrily refuses to wed, and braves her father's threats and violence to say so. Her mother too refuses to listen, and when Juliet turns to her Nurse for help, she receives only advice to conceal her love for Romeo and enter into an advantageous marriage with Paris (III, v).

In Act IV, Juliet, now forced to act on her own responsibility, goes to Friar Laurence for help. Arriving at his cell, she briefly meets Paris, who is arranging the forthcoming wedding. Juliet threatens to commit suicide rather than marry Paris, and, faced with this threat and with the discovery of his own unwise action in marrying the lovers, the Friar suggests a plan. Juliet is to take a potion which will make her seem as if dead. Once she is buried, Romeo, having been informed of the real state of affairs by Friar Laurence, will come to take her back to Mantua when she wakes (IV, i).

Juliet therefore returns home to apologize to her father and seemingly to prepare for the wedding, which is now brought forward to the following day, Wednesday (IV, ii).

That night, Juliet sends the Nurse away, and after many fearful thoughts finds the courage to drink the potion (IV, iii).

The following morning, her body is discovered by the Nurse and mourned both by her parents and by Paris, until Friar Laurence brings an end to the lamentation by conducting the body to the tomb (IV, iv; IV, v).

In Mantua, Romeo has been dreaming of Juliet. His servant, Balthasar, arrives from Verona. Having seen the funeral and not knowing the true story, he breaks to Romeo the news that Juliet is dead. Romeo immediately resolves to return to Verona and to die beside Juliet that night. He remembers a poor apothecary, whom he visits and bribes to provide him with poison (V, i).

We now discover that Friar Laurence has indeed sent a message to Romeo telling him what has really happened, but that the letter was delayed because of a plague in the town. Friar Laurence, believing that Romeo knows nothing of what has happened, decides to go himself to Juliet's tomb to be with her when she wakes (V, ii).

At the churchyard, Paris is keeping watch over Juliet's tomb. When he hears Romeo approaching, he withdraws. Romeo appears with Balthasar, whom he sends away with a letter to Lord Montague. Left alone, Romeo begins to open Juliet's tomb, but is stopped by Paris, who fears that he intends to do harm to the bodies. They fight, and Romeo kills Paris, although immediately afterwards he realizes who the man is and declares a bond with him. Romeo then opens Juliet's tomb and, after a final speech of love, drinks the poison and dies.

Friar Laurence arrives at the grave, meets Balthasar and learns that Romeo is there. Entering the tomb, the Friar discovers Paris and

Romeo, both dead. At that moment Juliet awakes and finds Romeo's corpse beside her. Friar Laurence tries to persuade her to leave the tomb, but she will not, and he runs away in fear. Seeing that Romeo has committed suicide, Juliet draws his dagger and kills herself too.

The play moves to its conclusion as the watchmen discover the bodies. The law, in the form of Prince Escalus, hears Friar Laurence, Paris's page and Balthasar give their accounts of what has happened. The tragedy reunites the two families, who propose to raise statues to the lovers. Prince Escalus speaks a final mourning speech (V, iii).

Scene-by-Scene Analysis

Prologue

The Prologue introduces the play. It is spoken by the Chorus, who is not a character but a spokesman for the company of actors. He outlines the basic plot: two children – 'A pair of star-crossed lovers' (l. 6), of opposing Veronese families – falling in love, an affair which ends in their death but reconciles the feuding families.

Notice that the Chorus's speech means that we already know the ending of the play, 'their death-marked love' (l. 9). This takes away the suspense but allows us to concentrate on the presentation and characterization of the play rather than wondering what will happen.

Notice too that the Chorus's speech is a sonnet, a fourteen-line poem often used for love lyrics. This is a classic way to present a section of a play separate from the rest. Right from the start it introduces us to the plot, the characters and the basic themes of love, fate, conflict and death.

Act I Scene i

The play opens by establishing in our minds the background atmosphere, by giving us actual proof of the feud – a quarrel and a fight. This also involves us from the start in exciting action.

Sampson and Gregory, of the Capulet family, enter talking angrily and defensively about their enemies the Montagues. They exchange puns and witty comments, but there is real viciousness behind the jokes, and when two Montagues appear, Sampson makes a rude gesture which provokes a fight. Peace-loving Benvolio of the Montague family tries to stop them, but Tybalt of the Capulet clan has by this time entered, delighted to have the opportunity to fight Benvolio. The brawl escalates to a full-blooded street battle between the two families.

At the battle's height, Prince Escalus, ruler of Verona, calls on the factions to stop fighting. He eventually makes himself heard – '. . . the Prince came, who parted either part' (l. 115) – and attempts to mediate between the heads of the two families, threatening the death penalty on anyone who fights again. His speech prepares us for his sentence of banishment on Romeo when violence erupts again in Act III.

As the streets clear, the Montagues gather to talk. Benvolio explains what has happened to Lord and Lady Montague. They also discuss Romeo, who, everyone agrees, has been depressed lately: 'Black and portentous must this humour prove' (l. 141). Benvolio has seen Romeo wandering in the woods before dawn, avoiding everyone. Lord Montague likens his son to a flower eaten away by the worm of self-indulgent melancholy. When Romeo appears, Benvolio suggests he talks to him and offers help.

At first Romeo parries Benvolio's questions, but he eventually admits to being hopelessly in love. He seems to wallow in his emotion, noticing the evidence of a fight but being too absorbed in his own problems to think of it for long. He speaks at length about 'love', comparing and contrasting various elements of it in what seems a forced and artificial manner: 'Feather of lead, bright smoke, cold fire, sick health' (l. 180).

Romeo will not tell Benvolio whom he loves, and at this stage we do not know that it is not Juliet. In fact he has not met her yet. He will only say that his beloved will not return his passion, 'She hath forsworn to love' (l. 223), which seems a waste of her beauty. She will not be tempted by words, glances or even presents. Benvolio advises his cousin that the way to overcome his suffering is to be attracted to other women: 'Examine other beauties' (l. 228). Although Romeo swears he could never love another, Benvolio takes up the challenge to prove him wrong. Does he succeed?

This scene, then, falls into two contrasting parts. The first explores the themes of conflict and potential death shown in the pointless feud, 'your cankered hate' (l. 95); it is motivated only by aggression and pride and only on the surface curbed by the law, represented by Prince Escalus's threat of death. The second part examines one aspect of love – self-indulgent romantic love. Both parts set the tense background atmosphere against which the tragedy is played out, and they combine to introduce us to the plot and seize our interest.

We also encounter the Montague family, particularly honest, peaceful Benvolio, and the Capulets, especially hot-headed Tybalt. The introduction of Tybalt here prepares us for the vital fight between Romeo and him in Act III. We also first hear of, then meet, Romeo. Why do you think Shakespeare keeps us waiting to meet the hero of the play?

From the start, Romeo seems a likeable, handsome and intelligent person. His family suspect him of self-indulgence, though, and when he appears we see him as someone who likes the attention he gets from being 'in love' but has as yet probably not felt the real emotion. When he does, of course, we see a different side of him.

Act I Scene ii

Lord Capulet is talking to Count Paris. They discuss the feud, but Paris is more eager to continue negotiating his proposed marriage to Lord Capulet's daughter. Capulet repeats that his daughter is not yet fourteen years old:

> *My child is yet a stranger in the world;*
> *She hath not seen the change of fourteen years.*   (ll. 8–9)

He feels that she is too young to marry successfully. If she agrees, however, he will allow the marriage. He suggests that Paris attends the Capulet feast to see if Juliet is really the one he wants.

In this part of the scene, we see another aspect of 'love' – the formal marriage proposal, made by Paris, a courteous young man who later in the play threatens the lovers' relationship. Lord Capulet, at this point in the play, seems to be genuinely concerned about his daughter's welfare: 'My will to her consent is but a part' (l. 17). We do not yet know, of course, that this daughter is Juliet.

The invitations for the feast mentioned by Lord Capulet are sent out with a servant, who cannot actually deliver them because he cannot read! He asks two passers-by for help – Romeo and Benvolio. At first Romeo teases the servant, but then is genuinely helpful. As he reads the guest list, however, he realizes that it includes Rosaline, his beloved.

Benvolio returns to his earlier suggestion and says they should gatecrash the feast and see how unattractive Rosaline seems beside others: 'And I will make thee think thy swan a crow' (l. 86). Romeo is aghast at the thought, speaking of his love as if it were a religion; he will never stop believing that Rosaline is more beautiful than anyone else. He does, however, agree to go to the feast, just to catch a glimpse of her.

In the second part of the scene, Romeo decides to go to the Capulet feast, a decision essential to the plot. Ironically, his reason for going is his passion for someone other than Juliet. Here we learn that his beloved is Rosaline. Romeo's love still seems overinflated, though we catch a glimpse of the more likeable side of Romeo in his good-natured teasing of the (Capulet) servant, followed by his helpfulness.

Notice how two further and opposing viewpoints of love are presented: the madness of Romeo's passion and Benvolio's easy-going attitude.

The whole scene involves us more in both families, as well as preparing the way for Paris's suit, with its tragic results, and for Romeo's attendance at the Capulet feast.

Act I Scene iii

The scene is the Capulet household. Lady Capulet, looking for her daughter, Juliet, asks the Nurse where she is. Juliet soon appears and respectfully greets her mother.

Lady Capulet wants to bring up the subject of marriage, but she is embarrassed. We have the impression that she is not close to her daughter and needs the Nurse present to make things easier. The Nurse embarks on a long and bawdy reminiscence about Juliet's childhood; how, when she was weaning, Juliet had fallen on her face, and had cried 'Yes' to the Nurse's husband's ribald comment that she would fall backwards (in love-making) when she was grown: 'Thou wilt fall backward when thou hast more wit' (l. 43). The Nurse repeats herself over and over, ceasing only when Juliet asks her to be quiet.

Lady Capulet pounces on the Nurse's reference to marriage. She tells her daughter that Paris wants to woo and marry her. But Juliet has not yet even considered marriage: 'It is an honour that I dream not of' (l. 67). Lady Capulet describes Paris in glowing terms, likening him to a book in need of a cover. She suggests that such a marriage would enrich Juliet in many ways, particularly in a financial sense: 'So shall you share all that he doth possess' (l. 94). Juliet obediently agrees to try to like Paris – 'I'll look to like, if looking liking move' (l. 98) – and, with the encouragement of both her mother and the Nurse, hurries off to the feast.

In this scene we meet the remaining members of the Capulet household. Lady Capulet is a rich, unlikeable woman. Her relationship with her daughter is distant, her interest in the marriage based on financial considerations, not on Juliet's happiness. Notice the high-flown language in her complex but emotionless description of Paris, typical of the conventional, financial view of love which she represents, and designed to persuade Juliet to come round to her point of view.

And Juliet is persuaded. Like Romeo, she is immature when we first meet her. At this stage she is willing to please her mother, even to the point of marrying as her mother wants, and is not yet ready to make her own decisions. It is ironic, though, that by the next day Juliet has married, and without her mother's consent.

We also see Juliet's good relationship with the Nurse, the warm affection they have for each other. The Nurse herself is a fine character-study of an older servant woman, who repeats coarse anecdotes but is genuinely warm-hearted.

The three women together present an interesting series of contrasts which lead us to further understanding of the role of women in the play.

Act I Scene iv

Romeo and his friends, led by the quick-witted Mercutio, are off to the Capulet's feast. Romeo is worried about explaining why they are there, for as Montagues they may be unwelcome. Benvolio says they will not bother to explain – the Capulets will just have to accept their presence.

Mercutio and Romeo exchange comments; Romeo is still depressed and will not join in the fun. Mercutio mocks him and his romantic expressions. Romeo is wary of going to the feast at all and explains that he had a worrying dream, and Mercutio again picks up his words to speak at length about dreams.

He talks of the fairy Queen Mab, first describing her and her carriage, then saying that she is the one who makes people dream of what they most want. He comments scornfully that most people dream of selfish things – money, passion, political success or the power to kill. The language and images he uses are disturbing, and it is obvious that Mercutio is working himself up into a frenzy.

Romeo interrupts him (l. 95), calming his friend, who suddenly comes out of his desperate mood, saying his fantasies are like a varying wind: 'I talk of dreams; Which are the children of an idle brain' (ll. 96–7). Benvolio, eager to reach the feast, urges everyone on; but Romeo, worried by his dream, and perhaps affected by Mercutio's mood, is still reluctant to go. He has a premonition of disaster (later proved all too true) which he fears will begin with the feast and end with his death:

> *Some consequence, yet hanging in the stars,*
> *Shall bitterly begin his fearful date*
> *With this night's revels . . .* (ll. 107–9)

But he is happy to leave that to God (fate). The group of friends go on to the Capulet feast.

As well as matching the knowledge we have of Juliet and her preparation for the feast with knowledge of Romeo's approach to it, this scene both introduces an important character, Mercutio, and creates atmosphere.

Mercutio, a relative of the Prince, is a lively, wild, seemingly depressive personality, the leader of the group and a friend of Romeo, who obviously cares for him. Mercutio's death later in the play is vital to the plot, as it drives the hero to murder.

Romeo himself has already sensed disaster ahead; the premonition, along with the disturbing effects of Mercutio's 'Queen Mab' speech, create a tense atmosphere. We know that Romeo is about to meet his love, but we are also made aware that he is about to begin a series of actions ending in his death. It is his choice, however, to go to the feast.

Act I Scene v

The preparations for the feast made by the four servingmen rushing around clearing furniture prepare us for the entrance of Lord and Lady Capulet, Tybalt and the guests.

Lord Capulet invites everyone to dance, remembering the days when he too was young enough to do so (ll. 22–5), chatting about this to a cousin.

Our attention then turns to Romeo (l. 42), who has just caught his first sight of Juliet, 'a snowy dove trooping with crows' (l. 48). He does not yet know who she is, but is captivated by her. He expresses his admiration in clear, genuine terms, praising Juliet by likening her to a jewel and a dove, immediately recognizing the difference between this attraction and what he felt for Rosaline, and plans to approach Juliet and touch her hand. She, we learn later, has seen him too.

Immediately, however, conflict accompanies love. Tybalt recognizes Romeo, and thinking that Romeo, a Montague, has gatecrashed for evil reasons, wants to kill him. Lord Capulet tries to stop him, first explaining that Romeo is a respected and virtuous young man, then – when Tybalt refuses to listen – berating him into submission. Tybalt seems to give in, 'Now seeming sweet, convert to bitterest gall' (l. 92), but in fact vows a revenge on Romeo which he later takes.

Romeo, meanwhile, has managed to approach Juliet and touch her hand. In fourteen lines of verse, they speak their first words to each other, a perfect sonnet which leads to their first kiss. The language and images are holy ones, reflecting the goodness of their love. Romeo is tentative but eager to kiss Juliet immediately; she, though arguing against, is willing, and enjoys the kiss: 'Then have my lips the sin that they have took' (l. 108). Then they kiss again. Their embrace is interrupted by the Nurse, who tells Romeo that Juliet is the daughter of the house; just as he learns the horrifying news that his love is a Capulet, Romeo is hurried away by Benvolio.

The feast draws to a close and the guests begin to leave. Juliet too wishes to know whom it is she has fallen in love with. She hides her real intention from the Nurse by asking the names of two other men before that of Romeo. She fears he is married, but when she learns the real truth, it is even more horrible: 'My only love, sprung from my only hate!' (l. 138). She does not renege on her feelings, though, and remains loyal to her attraction.

The scene in which Romeo and Juliet first meet is obviously a crucial one. It begins their romance; but the way in which Shakespeare juxtaposes it with Tybalt's aggression shows us clearly that it also begins the events which lead to their death.

The love we see here is very obviously romantic passion. Romeo's first instinct is to touch Juliet, and hers is to respond to his kiss. But unlike Romeo's indulgence for Rosaline, and unlike Juliet's proposed marriage, this love is also genuine; the religious language, the way the two respond to each other in complementing lines and the obvious instant equal attraction prove this.

Tybalt's anger at Romeo's presence – he very possibly notices Romeo's attraction to Juliet – contrasts superbly with this. Unlike the lovers, who seek unity, Tybalt wants to divide and destroy by aggression, even when challenged by Capulet, who also has to use force to control him. Tybalt is a living sign of the feud, present at the lovers' first meeting, and later he precipitates the tragedy by the revenge he wishes to take on Romeo. Tybalt reinforces our first impression of his impetuous character, and we begin to see how such hot-headedness runs in the family when Lord Capulet berates him. Tybalt's noticing Romeo at the feast is another example of the coincidences which run through the play.

Juliet too is impulsive. She responds to Romeo instinctively, without knowing who he is. Afterwards, she quickly learns to use deceit to find out. When she does discover that Romeo is a Montague, she is horrified but not deterred, and this reveals her strength of character.

Romeo at last finds his love. He reacts with physical affection, forgetting Rosaline easily; but he is aware of his about-turn. He also regards Juliet as holy, their love as a good force; and, indeed, from Lord Capulet's comments we learn that Romeo has a virtuous reputation.

Act II Scene i

The Chorus begins the Act with another sonnet; he comments on the passing of Romeo's old love and the start of his new. It is a dangerous love, though, for an enemy.

Romeo is unwilling to leave Juliet and the Capulet villa: 'Turn back, dull earth, and find thy centre out' (l. 2). He hears Benvolio and Mercutio coming, and withdraws to avoid them. They are eager to meet him. Benvolio is sure he jumped the wall of the Capulet villa. Mercutio, mocking Romeo's previous melancholy passion, pretends to conjure him up with a spell based on Rosaline's beauty: 'I conjure thee by Rosaline's bright eyes' (l. 7). He is full of bawdy jokes about Romeo's unrequited love and how Rosaline will not submit to his passion, but eventually Benvolio calms him and they abandon the search for Romeo and leave.

This scene reminds us of the bawdy side of love; Mercutio's rude jokes and sexual innuendo seem the very opposite of the 'holy' love Romeo spoke of; yet the physical basis is the same.

Mercutio is again seen as an intelligent yet cynical person, while Benvolio once more tries to make peace.

Act II Scene ii

Romeo, overhearing Mercutio's mockery, is angry. Soon, though, his attention is drawn by the sight of Juliet appearing at her balcony above: 'It is my lady. O, it is my love!' (l. 10). Romeo likens her to the sun rising, hoping that she will not be moon-like and chaste. He praises Juliet's beauty – her eyes, her cheeks – and wishes he were touching her.

Juliet sighs and, hearing her voice, Romeo immediately compares her to an angel. Juliet now speaks. She wonders where Romeo is, and whether he can reconcile their situation by renouncing his family:

> *be but sworn my love,*
> *And I'll no longer be a Capulet.* (ll. 35–6)

Then she ponders that it is only Romeo's name that is the problem, not himself or his physical presence, which is perfect.

Romeo moves forward at this. When Juliet, startled, asks who he is and then, recognizing his voice, calls him by name, he says that for her love he will give up his name.

Juliet, always practical, is afraid that Romeo may be caught by her avenging relatives. Romeo, still speaking in the high-flown language of love, answers each of her worried questions with a reassuring but conventional love image: 'And but thou love me, let them find me here' (l. 76).

Juliet is embarrassed at Romeo's having heard her declaration of 'my true-love passion' (l. 104) for him; but he has, so she abandons all pretence and asks him directly for a vow of love. She is wary of not playing love-games, feeling that Romeo will think her shallow and too easily won, but she promises her love is deep.

Romeo too swears his love, but Juliet is concerned that he swears by the changeable moon; she tells him to swear instead only by himself. She is worried about their meeting – it is so sudden that she fears it will die as suddenly: 'It is too rash, too unadvised, too sudden' (l. 118). When she begins to say good night, Romeo asks for Juliet's vow of love, which she gives gladly.

Then Juliet hears noises from within and goes inside, leaving Romeo so happy that he thinks he must be dreaming. Returning, Juliet is once more in a practical mood. She asks Romeo, if he wishes to marry her, to send her word tomorrow as to where and when the wedding will take place:

> *If that thy bent of love be honourable,*
> *Thy purpose marriage, send me word tomorrow.*   (ll. 143–4)

Distracted by the Nurse calling her, she adds that if he does not, he should go away and leave her to her 'grief' (l. 152). Sure of his love, she does not wait for his answer. Called by the Nurse, she then withdraws again.

Returning once more, Juliet softly calls Romeo back, regretting that she cannot shout his name. She asks when she should send for his message and promises to meet Romeo's request that she send at nine. She wants Romeo to stay near her; she is like someone who has a captive bird and lets it hop a little way off, only to recapture it again.

The lovers say good night, and Romeo is left alone, wishing he were with Juliet instead. Dawn is breaking and Romeo decides to visit Friar Laurence, his confessor, to tell him what has happened and ask for his help.

The 'balcony scene', as it is called, when Romeo and Juliet meet and are able to talk, is famous and quoted all too often; but despite this, try to read it as if for the first time.

The couple have no physical contact, even though they long to be together, but instead each has to begin to look at what the other is really like. They seem to complement each other, and the physical passion is matched by emotional tenderness, another side of love that up to now we have not been shown. It is Juliet's practicality that, by the end of the scene, moves them on to consider marriage as the natural end of such love.

The sense of conflict and the threat of death are still apparent, however, even in this romantic setting. Juliet's first words concern the division between them caused by the feud, and there is constant tension lest Romeo be discovered and killed.

It is once they are together that we begin to see Romeo's and Juliet's characters clearly and can watch them develop. Now that his love is reciprocated, Romeo's infatuation for Rosaline turns to a passionate tenderness for Juliet. Juliet moves quickly through girlish coyness to womanly eagerness for Romeo, and for fulfilment in marriage. She seems the stronger of the two, the more practical.

Act II Scene iii

Friar Laurence is Romeo's spiritual adviser. In the long opening speech we discover him to be a man in touch with nature, good-tempered and holy. The speech also reminds us of the essential paradox of nature: that good can result in evil, and vile things can bring good. Love, for Romeo and Juliet, results in death; but this death, seemingly a bad thing, has good results for their families. We are also reminded that later in the play Friar Laurence's knowledge of herbs takes on great importance.

Romeo enters, and the Friar realizes at once that he has been up all night, and guesses that this is because he has been depressed. Romeo, forgetting his previous distress about Rosaline, joyfully teases the Friar, refusing to tell him where he has spent the night.

Then Romeo directly tells the Friar how he has fallen in love with Juliet and how they wish the Friar to marry them today. Friar Laurence is taken aback; he accuses Romeo of a lack of emotional depth, a lack of strength, if he can grieve so much for Rosaline and then suddenly change his mind:

> *Young men's love then lies*
> *Not truly in their hearts, but in their eyes.*   (ll. 63–4)

Romeo, not distinguishing between infatuation and love, sulkily reminds the Friar that he himself said his feeling for Rosaline was a bad thing; surely this returned love is good.

Friar Laurence eventually agrees to help Romeo, hoping that if the young people marry this will help to heal the breach between their families, 'To turn your households' rancour to pure love' (l. 88).

This scene introduces into the play the power of the Church, characterized by Friar Laurence. He is a benevolent and devout man who understands Romeo, but he is also capable of power games. His opening speech not only shows us his knowledge of herbs, but introduces a premonition of death in the talk of poison.

Romeo's immaturity is shown clearly here: his stated justification for considering his love for Juliet good is that she returns his love. Friar Laurence's view of him as changeable and capable of infatuation further adds to our knowledge of Romeo's character.

Notice how, even at the start, Romeo's and Juliet's relationship is inextricably linked with the conflict of the feud. Friar Laurence's very reason for marrying the lovers is to reconcile their families. It does, but not in the way he expects.

Act II Scene iv

By now it is morning, and Mercutio and Benvolio are wondering where Romeo has been overnight. They are concerned because Tybalt has challenged Romeo to a duel, but Mercutio says that Romeo has already died from love of Rosaline and therefore Tybalt cannot harm him.

Mercutio's bright intelligence leads him on to a witty description of Tybalt and his skill at duelling, and in the middle of this Romeo enters. Mercutio teases him about having given them the slip last night; and Romeo immediately meets his teasing with jokes and puns of his own, so much so that Mercutio himself is lost for words. Romeo's friends are delighted at this change in him: 'Now thou art sociable. Now thou art Romeo' (l. 86). They think that he has fallen out of love and is 'normal' again: 'Why, is not this better now than groaning for love?' (l. 85).

As they are joking, the Nurse enters. The young men turn to teasing her bawdily, and although she pretends to be outraged, the Nurse quite enjoys it. When she finds out that one of the group is Romeo, she says she wants to speak to him privately, which causes great amusement among his friends, who nevertheless leave the pair alone. After complaining once more about Mercutio's behaviour, the Nurse speaks of Juliet. She is concerned in case Romeo's intentions are not honourable, 'a very gross kind of behaviour' (l. 163), although she hardly listens to his protests to the contrary. Romeo tells the Nurse to arrange for Juliet to come to Friar Laurence's cell that afternoon on the pretence of going to confession; the monk has agreed to marry them. Then Romeo arranges to visit Juliet in her room that night to celebrate the marriage. He offers to pay the Nurse, who, after a token protest, takes the money. She then begins to chatter on about Juliet, how pretty she is, how Paris wishes to marry her, but how much in love with Romeo she is. Romeo cuts the chatter short as the scene ends.

In this scene, then, Romeo meets again with his friends and seems a different person. Whereas his infatuation with Rosaline made him strange, depressed and self-indulgent, his love for Juliet makes him more himself, content and outgoing. He arranges the marriage with the Nurse discreetly and effectively and has regained much of his aristocratic bearing in dealing with her.

The Nurse herself is as bawdy and coarse as ever. The dialogue between herself and the salacious lads is evidence of this, and it also reminds us of the constant feuding between members of the two families, thus preparing us for the later fight. Notice how subtly we are reminded of Tybalt's increasing hatred towards Romeo by mention of the challenge which leads directly to the events in Act III, Scene i.

Act II Scene v

Juliet is worried and angry because the Nurse is late back from the meeting with Romeo. Bearers of messages of love should be swift; if the Nurse were young and in love, she would move quickly, but as it is, she is 'slow, heavy' (l. 17).

Then the Nurse arrives, and Juliet is wild for news. She is confused because the Nurse looks sad, and concludes that the news is bad. The Nurse leads Juliet on, complaining of weariness, praising Romeo, berating the girl for sending her on messages – doing everything in fact but giving Juliet the news she wants.

Juliet becomes irritated, but eventually pays the Nurse the attention she needs. At last, the servant comes to the point and tells Juliet of Romeo's plan for the marriage, and for his ascent to her room that night. Juliet is both delighted – 'Now comes the wanton blood up in your cheeks' (l. 70) – and eager, and runs off to Friar Laurence's cell, 'Hie to high fortune!' (l. 78).

Having looked at things from Romeo's viewpoint in the previous scene, we now turn to Juliet's. She handles the relationship on a far more emotional level than he, letting her eagerness and anger show. In the end, however, she is shrewd enough to play the Nurse's game in order to get what she wants. It is obvious how much in love Juliet is and how much her womanly passions have been aroused.

In contrast, the Nurse as an older woman still sees the whole affair as a game, and Juliet's emotions as something to be laughed at. She still has power over Juliet, and can, in her rough way, control her; it is with the Nurse's permission that Juliet goes to be married.

Act II Scene vi

Friar Laurence, about to perform the ceremony, prays that this marriage does not result in sorrow. (Is his prayer answered?) Romeo argues that even if it does he would think the marriage worthwhile.

> *But come what sorrow can*
> *It cannot countervail the exchange of joy*
> *That one short minute gives me in her sight.*   (ll. 3–5)

The Friar warns Romeo that strong emotions burn themselves out: 'Therefore love moderately. Long love doth so' (l. 14).

At that moment Juliet arrives, and for the first time since the feast she embraces Romeo. The Friar comments that lovers seem to walk on air. They greet each other with classical lovers' language, expressing how happy they are to meet, and how rich in emotion. The Friar then hurries to marry them immediately.

We do not see the actual marriage of Romeo and Juliet, although some productions of the play follow this scene by a mimed wedding. Instead, we see the passionate eagerness of the lovers to be with each other, and Friar Laurence's attempt to make this passion holy by marrying them.

Even at this, the blessing of their love, we are reminded of tragedy by the Friar's warning and by Romeo's death-defying words.

Act III Scene i

Benvolio warns Mercutio that the day is so hot and everyone in such a bad mood that there is bound to be a fight, 'For now, these hot days, is the mad blood stirring' (l. 4), and suggests that perhaps they ought to go home. Mercutio accuses Benvolio himself of being a troublemaker – is this true? – and says that it is Benvolio who will start a fight at any excuse.

As they speak, Tybalt and the Capulets enter. Tybalt still wants revenge on Romeo, and as Romeo is not to be found, picking a fight with Romeo's friends is the next best thing. Mercutio replies wittily to Tybalt's challenge, and seems himself ready for a fight, while Benvolio tries to persuade them to talk logically, in private, rather than urging each other on to a fight.

Mercutio will not move, and Tybalt, seeing Romeo approach (direct from his marriage to Juliet), turns his attention there. He addresses Romeo, 'thou art a villain' (l. 60), but Romeo calmly ignores the insult and, because Juliet's family is now as important to him as his own, speaks kindly to the Capulet:

> *Tybalt, the reason that I have to love thee*
> *Doth much excuse the appertaining rage*
> *To such a greeting.*   (ll. 61–3)

Mercutio is outraged by Romeo's apparent capitulation, 'O calm, dishonourable, vile submission' (l. 72), draws his sword and challenges Tybalt to fight. Romeo tries to stop them, first by persuasive words, then by reminding them of Prince Escalus's edict. While Romeo is trying to part them as they fight, Tybalt wounds Mercutio, under Romeo's arm.

Knowing that he has fatally wounded Mercutio, Tybalt runs away. Mercutio's friends, however, do not realize what has happened. They see that Tybalt has been beaten. Mercutio merely says, 'I am hurt . . . a scratch' (ll. 90 & 93), and follows with a series of jokes about wounds and death, at which his friends laugh: 'They have made worms' meat of me' (l. 107).

Gradually, however, as the realization of the seriousness of the wound grows, Mercutio's tone changes. He rails at Tybalt, at the feud, at the two families, and rebukes Romeo for coming between them, allowing Tybalt to strike the blow. With a final curse on 'both your houses', Mercutio leaves. Benvolio enters a moment after with news of his death.

Romeo, now aware of what has happened, is overcome with grief and anger. He has allowed himself to be influenced by his love for Juliet, thereby losing his courage and the urge to defend his honour. He regrets this and at this point, so soon after the marriage, seems also to regret his love.

Tybalt returns. Seeing him alone, Romeo finds his grief for Mercutio turning to anger. He now answers Tybalt's previous challenge with his own threat: that either he or Tybalt must die. They fight, and Romeo kills Juliet's cousin. As soon as he has slain Tybalt, Romeo realizes what he has done: 'O, I am fortune's fool!' (l. 136). Urged on by Benvolio he flees, and it is Benvolio who has to face the wrath of Prince Escalus.

The Prince enters, demanding to know who began the fight. This is the second of the three times in the play where Escalus arbitrates between the two families. Interrupted by cries for revenge from Lady Capulet, Benvolio tells everything, showing Romeo in a good light. He relates how Romeo tried to make peace with Tybalt, who nevertheless attacked Mercutio. Then, wishing to part them, how Romeo stepped between the pair, and inadvertently gave Tybalt the opening to kill Mercutio. Finally, Benvolio stresses how Romeo only then thought of revenge, and only when Tybalt had again challenged him.

Lady Capulet argues that Benvolio's explanation is biased, and demands the death of Romeo in return for Tybalt's. The Prince, however, caps this by pointing out that Tybalt first killed Mercutio. But although Romeo thus escapes the death penalty, the Prince declares him exiled and the families fined. The Prince is particularly angry because one of his kinsmen, Mercutio, has been killed, and his final lines show that he is determined to stop the feud: 'Mercy but murders, pardoning those that kill' (l. 197).

The theme of conflict is closely examined in this scene, which, with its exciting but tragic fight, marks both the mid-point and turning-point of the play. We see how heated emotions lead to violence, how violence leads to death. We also see that the law – represented by Prince Escalus – is ineffectual and cannot really control what is happening.

Romeo's new-found love at first makes him meet Tybalt's challenge with gentleness. He genuinely tries to stop the fight. His friend's death, however, engenders a desire for revenge. He blames Juliet, reneging on his love, and also curses fate, but it is his own impetuosity that leads him to kill Tybalt and brings about his own banishment. The killing begins the downward turn of events which ends in tragedy.

The other characters behave in the manner that we would now expect of them: Mercutio dies exhibiting the same wit and aggression that led into the fight, and uttering a curse on the families which, of course, comes true; Tybalt displays the same hot-headedness. The families continue to feud despite the fatal consequences of their aggression. Only Benvolio tries to be a peacemaker.

The deaths in this scene, the first in the play, not only provide us with dramatic excitement, but also prepare us for the later tragedy. Shakespeare makes sure that neither has the emotional impact of the lovers' deaths by having Mercutio joke about his wound and die off-stage, and by having Tybalt die quickly, his death overshadowed by the sympathy we feel for Romeo.

Act III Scene ii

Juliet waits for Romeo to arrive to consummate their marriage. She longs for night to fall, so that Romeo may come to her in secret. Juliet is eager to lose her maidenhead and to learn the arts of love: 'learn me how to lose a winning match' (l. 12). She likens Romeo to snow, then to stars in the heavens, outshining the sun. She has been wed, but now longs for the night so that she may be truly married. Remember that while we hear Juliet's hopes, we know the reality of the situation – that her husband has killed her cousin and is exiled.

The Nurse comes in with the cords which Romeo is to use to enter Juliet's room. She is distraught because she bears news of Tybalt's death, repeating 'he's dead' over and over. Juliet immediately thinks it is Romeo who is dead, and questions the Nurse, who describes the wound she saw on the pale corpse. At this, Juliet, convinced of Romeo's death, breaks down with grief.

It is then that the Nurse begins to mourn for Tybalt by name, and Juliet, confused, asks if both Romeo and her cousin are dead. The Nurse now explains herself clearly:

> *Tybalt is gone, and Romeo banished;*
> *Romeo that killed him, he is banished.*   (ll. 69–70)

At this news, Juliet turns on Romeo. She accuses him of hiding his true nature, which she now sees as violent, albeit with an outward show of attractiveness:

> *O serpent heart, hid with a flowering face!*   (l. 73)

> *A damnèd saint, an honourable villain!*   (l. 79)

The Nurse joins in Juliet's anger, cursing all men as evil, and ending: 'Shame come to Romeo!' (l. 90). Juliet turns on her immediately, defending her husband and regretting her own harsh words: 'Upon his brow shame is ashamed to sit' (l. 92). She thinks through the situation, now almost calmly, and realizes that Romeo was only defending himself against Tybalt and that, had he had not done so, he would have died himself, a far worse blow to her. She also realizes that though Tybalt's death is tragic, it is the fact that Romeo is banished that is the worse news. It is as if all her family were dead, that her love is now gone for ever. Rather than weep over Tybalt's corpse, Juliet prefers to mourn Romeo: 'No words can that woe sound' (l. 126).

Convinced she will never see him again, Juliet orders the Nurse to remove the cords because they are useless now. The Nurse, however, suggests she finds Romeo, and, handing her a ring to give him, Juliet joyfully agrees that they should say a final good-bye before his banishment: 'And bid him come to take his last farewell' (l. 143).

In this scene we see Juliet's reaction to what has happened. Her almost childish anticipation of her wedding night soon turns to anger at the Nurse's unclear message, and then to real grief at the thought of Romeo's death. When she hears the true version of events, Juliet at first blames Romeo, but almost immediately moves through this to a greater maturity in which she logically and forcefully assesses the situation and sees the best in it.

Juliet's love for Romeo is obvious. Even when she is blaming him, she praises his attractiveness and soon defends him to the Nurse and welcomes him to her bed. True love accepts, not rejects, the beloved, whatever happens. However, even true love cannot remain untouched by the realities of life. The lovers cannot escape the immediacy of the feud of death.

Act III Scene iii

Meanwhile, Romeo is in hiding at Friar Laurence's cell. The Friar brings Romeo news of the Prince's judgement on him, banishment, which the priest sees as a merciful sentence.

Romeo, however, is desperate. He says he would rather die than be banished from Verona: 'Be merciful, say "death"' (l. 12). Banishment is in fact a death sentence for him.

The Friar tells Romeo he is ungrateful, since the Prince has commuted the death sentence he should have suffered. But Romeo argues that Juliet is in Verona – and every animal there, even the flies, can see her and are therefore luckier than he is. He accuses the Friar of cruelty, of killing him, by bringing him the news of his banishment.

The Friar tries to reason with Romeo, who will not listen at all. He accuses his confessor of not understanding the situation: if Laurence were in Romeo's place, 'Wert thou as young as I' (l. 66), he too would be desperate.

When a knock comes at the door, Friar Laurence wants Romeo to hide, but Romeo wants to be discovered. In fact it is the Nurse, who, seeing Romeo, comments that Juliet is weeping too and encourages him to stand up and be manful. Romeo is worried about what Juliet now thinks of him:

> *and what says*
> *My concealed lady to our cancelled love?*   (ll. 97–8)

The Nurse replies that Juliet is distressed, whereupon Romeo becomes desperate and reaches for the Friar's knife in order to stab himself.

This causes the Friar to finally lose patience. He asks Romeo if he is truly a man, for he does not behave like one. Killing himself would only destroy Juliet and the love they share: 'Killing that love which thou hast vowed to cherish' (l. 129). He tells Romeo to remember the good things: Juliet is alive, as he himself is; Tybalt, his enemy, no longer threatens him; he is not to be executed but merely banished. Romeo should be grateful, not miserable.

Friar Laurence tells Romeo to go to Juliet that night, then leave the city the following day and go to Mantua until everything can be reconciled and Romeo summoned back. He arranges for Romeo's servant to keep him informed of what is happening. By this time Romeo has come to his senses and is ready to follow the Friar's advice. He takes the ring which Juliet sent and hurries off to join her.

Compare Romeo's reactions in this scene to those of Juliet, and see what you learn about their characters. Romeo's reaction is desperate and self-indulgent; he is ready to commit suicide rather than face banishment, an action which prepares us for his later, successful suicide.

This may well show how strong his love is, but is he thinking of Juliet at all when he does this? It is not until the Friar talks him through his desperation and he comes to the same set of realizations Juliet has reached by herself that he achieves perspective on the situation.

The Friar is seen in his best light in this scene: he appears as sensible, strong and able to think clearly and help Romeo. He represents maturity, as does the Nurse when she stops Romeo killing himself. The attempted suicide is yet another horror piled on what has happened and leads us to the final tragedy; but in the middle of this horror the lovers are meanwhile preparing for the consummation of their marriage.

Act III Scene iv

Lord Capulet is apologizing to Paris because, owing to Tybalt's death, the proposed courtship of Juliet has not progressed. Paris courteously bids the Capulets good night, but Lord Capulet suddenly makes an offer of Juliet's hand:

> *a desperate tender*
> *Of my child's love.*   (ll. 12–13)

He is sure Juliet will agree if he, her father, tells her to. Capulet suggests Thursday for the marriage and a small feast for the wedding party, because of the mourning for Tybalt. He tells his wife to break the news to Juliet immediately.

Paris, whom we have not seen since Act I, Scene ii, is now re-introduced, a serious threat to the lovers' happiness. In order that the action of the play moves swiftly, it is important that the marriage threat be imminent; hence the decision to set the wedding for Thursday. Paris himself remains an undefined character, the classically romantic lover. Lord Capulet, who previously appeared to be considerate of his daughter's feelings, now seems prepared to override them in order to marry her to Paris.

Notice the contrast between this arranged loveless marriage and the love-based one being consummated at the same time.

Act III Scene v

Romeo and Juliet have spent the night together and celebrated their marriage, and now Romeo is preparing to leave. Juliet is convinced he does not need to go yet, for it is not really dawn (compare this with the way she wanted him to speed on in Act III, Scene ii). Romeo assures her that it is dawn – the lark is singing and the sky is lightening, 'I must be gone and live, or stay and die' (l. 11).

Juliet argues that it is not the lark they hear, and that the light they see is only a meteor. She begs her husband to stay. Impetuously he agrees to do so, if that is what Juliet wants. But then, with the sudden realization of danger at hand, Juliet fears for his life and urges him to go.

The Nurse hurries in to warn Juliet that Lady Capulet is coming to her soon, to which Juliet replies: 'let day in, and let life out' (l. 41). Hastily, Romeo climbs down from the balcony, while Juliet urges him to write to her often. The lovers say their last farewells. Juliet is suddenly unaccountably afraid that Romeo will die before she sees him again; he looks pale. Romeo comforts her by saying that she does too, 'Dry sorrow drinks our blood' (l. 59), and after a brief adieu he leaves. Juliet curses Fortune for taking Romeo away, and then turns back into the house to greet her mother.

Lady Capulet begins by criticizing Juliet for her continued tears, which she assumes are still for Tybalt and against his murderer. Juliet, speaking with a series of double meanings, assures her mother that, yes, Tybalt's murderer Romeo, does make her unhappy: 'And yet no man like he doth grieve my heart!' (l. 83). In response to this, Lady Capulet assures her daughter that there is a plan to poison Romeo in revenge for the killing. Though aghast, Juliet keeps her head sufficiently to keep up the pretence of hating Romeo, and further manages to protect Romeo by offering herself to arrange the poisoning.

Lady Capulet now turns the conversation to the marriage which she and Lord Capulet have arranged for Juliet and Paris. Juliet's reaction is direct and angry. For the first time, she refuses to obey her mother: 'He shall not make me there a joyful bride!' (l. 117). She argues that Paris has not wooed her yet.

Lady Capulet, helpless, turns to her husband, who has entered and is exclaiming at Juliet's tears. He likens her to a storm-tossed ship. When he hears Juliet's response, however, his sympathy goes, and he turns on her, calling her ungrateful and proud. When Juliet answers him back, refusing the marriage but expressing her thanks, he directly orders her to wed Paris or else be dragged to the church.

Both Lady Capulet and the Nurse protest at these harsh words, but this merely increases Lord Capulet's anger. He rants on – how he has cared for Juliet, how he is concerned that she makes a good marriage:

> *my care hath been*
> *To have her matched.* (ll. 178–9)

Now that he has done so, he complains, his care is rejected. He states his position clearly: if Juliet is his daughter, he may marry her off; if not, he has no responsibility for her and she may starve. He storms off.

Juliet turns in desperation to her mother, begging her to delay the marriage, but Lady Capulet is implacable: 'I have done with thee' (l. 204).

Juliet's final hope is her Nurse, and tearfully she asks her for advice – her position seems impossible. The Nurse answers Juliet with common-sense. Romeo is banished and cannot return to claim her, she argues. Therefore it seems more sensible to marry Paris, who seems even more attractive than Romeo, and is a better match: 'I think it best you married with the County' (l. 218).

Stunned by the Nurse's reply, Juliet realizes that everyone has deserted her. She takes her own decision, telling the Nurse that she has repented of her behaviour and is going to Friar Laurence to be absolved of her sin.

When the Nurse has gone, Juliet curses her for her wicked, heartless advice, and swears that from now on she will never trust the Nurse: 'Thou and my bosom henceforth shall be twain' (l. 241). She goes off to Friar Laurence to seek his advice – or if he fails her, to kill herself.

In this scene the lovers see each other for the last time alive and are then thrust back into the real world of real problems. Their love has been consummated; they seem more mature, truly at one. Romeo is now content to go to Mantua to cope with the problems of banishment. Juliet, whose premonition of death is all too accurate, is left to handle first the proposed murder of Romeo, then her own suggested marriage. She acts emotionally but effectively in both situations. She also gains full autonomy when all her close family betray her: she withdraws into herself and then reaches a mature decision, choosing what she knows to be right.

Her parents show little affection for Juliet. Her mother is cold and withdrawn; her father's anger is motivated by a drive for her welfare, but he is impetuous and vicious. The Nurse chooses the most sensible solution to the problem, but also shows her double standards and insensitivity. Juliet responds by withdrawing her affection from the Nurse and for the first time treats her as a servant.

After the high point of the lovers' relationship, their love-making, everything now begins to go wrong for them. The feud returns to their lives in Lady Capulet's planned revenge, another example of the death that haunts the play, and, of course, Romeo does die through poison. The planned marriage is now a real threat, and leads on to the coming events.

Act IV Scene i

Paris is at Friar Laurence's cell, arranging the marriage. Friar Laurence, for his own reasons, is trying to persuade the Count to postpone the marriage. Paris replies that it is Lord Capulet's wish, in order to stop Juliet grieving too much for Tybalt.

At this moment Juliet arrives. Paris greets her as his wife, 'my lady and my wife' (l. 18), and the two indulge in some light-hearted banter. Juliet then gently dismisses Paris by turning to Friar Laurence and asking to see him alone, and Paris courteously makes his exit.

Once alone with Friar Laurence, Juliet pours out her grief, begging him to help her avoid the marriage to Paris. She (like Romeo in Act III, Scene iii) threatens to stab herself if he cannot help. She reminds him that to some extent he is responsible for the situation, having aided them in the marriage.

The Friar now sees 'a kind of hope' (l. 68). If Juliet is brave enough to kill herself, then she may have the courage to attempt the solution he offers. Juliet answers immediately that she would rather undergo anything than betray Romeo by marrying Paris:

> *O, bid me leap, rather than marry Paris,*
> *From off the battlements of any tower.*   (ll. 77–8)

She is even prepared to go into a 'new-made grave' (l. 84).

Friar Laurence intervenes. If Juliet is willing, he suggests she should agree to marry Paris; but the night before the wedding (here Wednesday, though it is later changed), she is to send the Nurse away. Juliet should drink the potion the Friar gives her. After a while, her heartbeat and breathing will stop. Her family, thinking her dead, will place her in an open tomb. Forty-two hours later, she will wake, as if she had only been asleep. Meanwhile, the Friar will have informed Romeo of what has happened and he will return to take her back to Mantua. Juliet is eager to follow his plan, 'Love give me strength, and strength shall help afford' (l. 125), and the Friar gives her the potion, promising to write to Romeo.

This scene divides into two halves. In the first, the arranged marriage proceeds. Juliet and Paris meet, and their formally courteous conversation contrasts with the passionate communication we have seen between the lovers. In the second half, the desperation that this arranged marriage has created in Juliet leads to the next step in the tragedy. We see how her love for Romeo enables her to brave even the most macabre situation.

Juliet herself continues to mature. She shows great emotional strength in her actions, as well as a shrewdness that leads her to deceive Paris and shame the Friar into helping her.

Paris is, as ever, courteous and devoted, though a little possessive here. The Friar begins to be seen in a worse light than before – he knows he has done wrong in arranging the marriage, and we are unsure whether he now wants to help Juliet or conceal his own actions.

Act IV Scene ii

Capulet is organizing the wedding feast. He asks where Juliet is, and at that moment she enters, greets her father meekly and begs his pardon for her disobedience:

> *I have learnt me to repent the sin*
> *Of disobedient opposition.*   (ll. 17–18)

She adds that, while at Friar Laurence's cell, she met Paris and encouraged him: 'And gave him what becomèd love I might' (l. 26).

Capulet is delighted, taking his daughter back into favour again and sending news of the marriage to Paris. He decides to bring the wedding forward to Wednesday, and overrules his wife's objections. Juliet and the Nurse go to lay out her trousseau, while Capulet stays up all night preparing the wedding, happy that his daughter has repented: 'this same wayward girl is so reclaimed' (l. 47).

Here we see the continuing preparations for the wedding which, after Juliet's agreement, is now brought forward, increasing the threat to the lovers, and of course disturbing Friar Laurence's plan.

Capulet is like a child, scurrying round arranging matters, delighted (and deceived) when Juliet apologizes, eager for the wedding. Juliet has now completely gained her emotional independence from her parents and the Nurse, and lies to them convincingly.

Act IV Scene iii

Juliet and the Nurse are preparing the wedding clothes. Lady Capulet comes to help. Juliet sends them away, however, first saying that she needs to pray, then that they must have other things to do.

Left alone, Juliet prepares to take the potion. She is afraid: 'I have a faint cold fear thrills through my veins' (l. 15). She begins to call the Nurse, but stops, resolute in her action. She worries that the potion may not work and that the Friar may intend to kill her and so protect his reputation. Then she fears that she will wake in the tomb before Romeo comes, and will have to gaze on Tybalt's corpse and the other horrors of the grave, which will send her mad: 'shall I not be distraught' (l. 49). Frightened, Juliet thinks she sees Tybalt's ghost seeking revenge on Romeo, and in sudden panic and desire to be with her love she drinks the potion: 'I drink to thee' (l. 59).

This scene, where Juliet drinks the potion, shows her great strength of character. In going through with the plan, alone, she shows how she has gained real maturity through the course of the play. She also shows fear and desperation. Her speech not only whips the audience into the same hysteria she feels, but builds the atmosphere of impending doom even further. The images she uses are macabre and increase our sense of the horror of what she is doing.

Juliet's motivation is her love for Romeo; it is her last fantasy, of Romeo being in danger, that finally drives her to drink the potion.

Act IV Scenes iv & v

It is morning. Lady Capulet and the Nurse are preparing food for the wedding feast. Capulet is distractedly rushing round organizing the servingmen, despite the Nurse's warning that he will make himself ill.

Music announces the arrival of Paris, and Capulet sends the Nurse to waken Juliet while he chats to the Count. The Nurse draws back the curtains on Juliet's bed and calls her affectionately. She comments that Juliet sleeps now because, once married, she will have little rest: 'Ay, let the County take you in your bed' (v, l. 10).

Suddenly, the Nurse realizes that Juliet is dead. She shrieks and calls for her master and mistress. Lord and Lady Capulet react as one would expect to the death of their daughter, as does Paris, who enters with Friar Laurence. What follows reveals their characters, as they mourn Juliet with more or less sincerity. Capulet says:

> *Death lies on her like an untimely frost*
> *Upon the sweetest flower of all the field.*   (v, ll. 28–9)

Lady Capulet adds her lament, saying she regrets the loss of the daughter whom, in the previous Act, she disowned. Capulet, while claiming that grief makes him speechless, speaks at length on the tragedy of Juliet's dying on her wedding day, and how this leaves him with no reason to live: 'Death is my son-in-law. Death is my heir' (v, l. 38). Paris too speaks with conventional if sincere grief, while the Nurse shrieks her sorrow.

All of them seem more concerned with their own reactions than with Juliet's state, and this self-indulgence is interrupted by Friar Laurence. He reminds them that, if they truly loved Juliet and were concerned with her well-being, they would wish her in heaven, with eternal life:

> *you love your child so ill*
> *That you run mad, seeing that she is well.*   (v, ll. 75–6)

Instead, all they wanted for her was a good marriage; they should cease crying and bear Juliet's corpse to church.

Capulet comments that they are now turning all the wedding festivities to funeral solemnities, and at this the Friar suggests that everyone prepares to follow the body to the graveyard.

The final section of the scene is a humorous interlude in which three of the wedding musicians and Peter joke and bandy words. This helps to lift the gloom after the deep, but misplaced, mourning over Juliet, and prepares us for the final unfolding of the real tragedy.

This scene, where Juliet's body is discovered, shows us conventional grief over death, shallow love expressed with conventional words. Those who mourn for Juliet, with the possible exception of Paris, who later defends her body with his life, do not seem to do so with genuinely selfless love. Compare their reactions to Romeo's in Act V, Scene i. It is Friar Laurence who reminds them what real love is, although, ironically, he knows (as we do) that what they are mourning is not real death. It is, nevertheless, a further horror to prepare us for the coming tragedy.

Act V Scene i

Romeo, who is in Mantua, feels optimistic – 'My dreams presage some joyful news at hand' (l. 2) – after a dream that Juliet's kisses revived him when he was dead. Why is this ironic?

Balthasar, his servant, arrives from Verona, and Romeo immediately asks for news of Juliet. Balthasar at first reassures his master, then blurts out that he knows Juliet is dead – he has seen her buried: 'Her body sleeps in Capel's monument' (l. 18). Romeo's reaction is characteristically emotional: 'Then I defy you, stars!' (l. 24). He tells Balthasar, who is understandably worried, that he is not going to do anything rash, then orders him to arrange their departure that night.

But Romeo has indeed decided to join Juliet in death: 'Well, Juliet, I will lie with thee tonight' (l. 34). He wonders how to do so, and then remembers a poor apothecary, whose shop he has visited and who seems the sort of man who would sell him poison. Romeo offers the apothecary forty ducats to provide him with a fatal poison, and overrides the apothecary's misgivings by pointing out his poverty. Handing over the money, he comments that gold does more harm than poison: 'I sell thee poison. Thou hast sold me none' (l. 83). Romeo sets off to join his love.

Upon receiving the news of Juliet's supposed death (we do not yet know why Romeo has not heard the true story from the Friar), Romeo reacts by planning to kill himself too. His love, though emotional, is clearly shown here, as it is in his joyful dream about Juliet.

Like Juliet, Romeo is now acting on his own behalf. His cry 'Then I defy you, stars!' shows that he intends to take his fate into his own hands. We now see a world-weary Romeo whose only aim is to end his life and join Juliet. However, we also see a strong man, who can follow his own decisions without support, and a kind one, who sees to it that the apothecary is well paid.

That Romeo has had the wrong information is a direct cause of his suicide – one example of the many coincidences which run through the play.

Act V Scene ii

Friar John arrives at Friar Laurence's cell. We learn immediately that he was the bearer of Laurence's message to Romeo. However, while trying to find another monk to accompany him to Mantua, he became suspected of plague infection and was kept in quarantine. He has not been to Mantua, nor was he able to send the vital letter.

Friar Laurence is worried: 'Unhappy fortune!' (l. 17). Sending Friar John for a crowbar to open the tomb, he decides to go himself to comfort Juliet when she wakes, and keep her hidden till Romeo can fetch her: 'Poor living corpse, closed in a dead man's tomb!' (l. 29).

The reason why Romeo has not received news of the truth of Juliet's burial now becomes clear. It is pure chance that Friar John cannot deliver the letter, chance that leads to the final act of the tragedy. Friar Laurence reacts with typical practicality and commits a further deception in order to cover his previous deceitful acts.

Act V Scene iii

It is night-time. Paris has come to visit Juliet's grave in secret. He tells his servant to keep watch and warn him if anyone approaches. Paris strews Juliet's tomb with flowers, as her marriage bed would have been, and promises to do this for her every night: 'Nightly shall be to strew thy grave and weep' (l. 17). Then he hears his page's whistle and withdraws.

The page is warning of the arrival of Romeo and Balthasar. Romeo tells his servant first to deliver a letter to Lord Montague the next morning, and secondly not to interfere, whatever he sees Romeo doing, or Romeo will tear him limb from limb. He says to Balthasar that he is only visiting Juliet's tomb to see her and take a ring from her finger. When the servant agrees, Romeo wishes him well and gives him money: 'Live, and be prosperous' (l. 42). Balthasar is still concerned, however, and hides nearby to keep watch.

Romeo turns to the tomb, likening it to a wild animal that has eaten

Juliet: 'I'll cram thee with more food' (l. 48). He begins to open the tomb when he is challenged by Paris, who, knowing Romeo to be the killer of Tybalt, fears he is about to desecrate the tomb. Romeo sees Paris, greets him kindly and advises him not to interfere, for if he does, Romeo will have to kill him, which he does not want to do. Paris continues to defend the tomb, Romeo and he fight, and Paris dies, with a final plea to be buried next to Juliet. His page, seeing all this, rushes off to find the Watchman.

Romeo suddenly realizes who Paris is – the man who should have married Juliet. He takes Paris's hand, feeling at one with him in their common unhappiness: 'One writ with me in sour misfortune's book' (l. 82). Then he opens the tomb, and places Paris in it.

Romeo is now reunited with Juliet and prepares to die. He feels happy, as men often do before execution, as he gazes on Juliet's face, marvelling that death has not affected her beauty, the colour in her lips and cheeks:

> *Death, that hath sucked the honey of thy breath,*
> *Hath had no power yet upon thy beauty.*   (ll. 92–3)

What is the irony in this statement? How might it affect the audience?

Romeo now turns to the corpse of Tybalt, now to be avenged by Romeo's suicide. Then he turns back to Juliet's unmarred beauty – perhaps Death is keeping her to be his lover. But now Romeo will stay with her to protect her from that. He gazes at Juliet, embraces and kisses her one last time:

> *seal with a righteous kiss*
> *A dateless bargain to engrossing death!*   (ll. 114–15)

He is weary of life and, like a boat ready to be dashed on the rocks, is near to death. He drinks the potion as if it were a toast to Juliet. It works speedily and he dies kissing his beloved.

Friar Laurence, on his way to the tomb, meets Balthasar, who tells him that Romeo is there and that he 'dreamed' that Romeo fought and killed someone else. Frightened now, the Friar approaches, sees the blood and weapons, enters the tomb and finds the bodies of both Romeo and Paris.

Juliet awakes, at first content to see the Friar and know the plan has worked. She looks for Romeo, whose body at first she does not see.

The Friar urges her out of the vault, saying that their plans have been thwarted: Romeo is dead, and so is Paris. Afraid and eager to be gone, he suggests that he takes Juliet to sanctuary in a convent. But Juliet refuses, and the Friar flees.

Left alone with her love, Juliet realizes that he has taken poison. Desperate to die and be united with him, she first tries to drain the bottle of poison, which is empty, then kisses his lips in the hope of poisoning herself that way. She is distraught to find that Romeo's lips are still warm. Then, disturbed by the noise of the Watchman approaching, Juliet seizes Romeo's dagger and stabs herself: 'This is thy sheath; there rust, and let me die' (l. 170).

The lovers are dead, reunited, and the tragedy is over. What follows seems an anti-climax, but is necessary to complete the story by making public what has happened and reuniting the families.

Paris's page shows the Watchman the site of the tomb. After searching, they find Paris, Romeo and Juliet newly dead. Prince Escalus and the Capulet and Montague families are summoned, and Balthasar and the Friar are taken into custody. The Prince arrives, and then the Capulets, who hear the news with horror. Lord Montague, who announces the death of his wife, is equally moved.

The Prince now demands to know what has happened, for the sake of justice, and the Friar is first to speak. He accuses himself of having partly caused the tragedy, and briefly tells the story of the marriage, and the effect of Tybalt's death and Romeo's banishment on the lovers, how Juliet persuaded him to give her the potion, and how news of this failed to reach Romeo. He ends by explaining the events after he reached the tomb, and finally offers his life as forfeit for his responsibility in what has happened:

> *let my old life*
> *Be sacrificed . . .*   (ll. 267–8)

Balthasar tells how he brought Romeo news of Juliet's death and accompanied him back to the vault, and then the page relates how he saw Paris and Romeo fight. Romeo's letter to his father confirms all that has been said, and so Prince Escalus judges that no further action should be taken, all involved having been punished, including himself for his leniency.

Lords Capulet and Montague join hands, agreeing to make statues of the lovers to honour them and signify the end of the feud: 'I will raise her statue in pure gold' (l. 299). The Prince speaks the last words of sorrow at the story of the lovers:

> *For never was a story of more woe*
> *Than this of Juliet and her Romeo.* (ll. 309–10)

The climax of the tragedy, though known to us before, is still moving. The tension mounts with Romeo's arrival and his fight with Paris, followed by the final acts of love contained in the double suicide. Both Romeo and Juliet die because they cannot bear to be without each other, to them the highest expression of their passion. Because of this the conflict is ended and the families are reconciled; but it is a bitter victory, for it has taken death to end death – the death not only of the lovers, but of Paris and Lady Montague.

Even here, fate (or chance) still operates: it disturbs us, while at the same time adding to the dramatic impact, that Romeo chances to kill himself just before Juliet wakes.

The lovers gain honour they have not previously found. Both have matured, Juliet more than Romeo, and choose their deaths knowingly, if unwisely, firm and unswayed in their resolution, each considering love of the other to be more important than living. Beside this, Paris's formal though genuine affection seems lifeless, and the mourning of their families merely a postscript.

However, by the end of the play, all have learned a lesson. The parents now mourn truly for their children and we feel they will indeed do their best to end the feud. The Friar admits his mistake and, for that, is pardoned. Prince Escalus, the representative of law and order, realizes that his weakness is as much to blame as the families for what has happened.

The final lines close the play on a note of sorrow, and are spoken not by the family but by Escalus. Although the lovers' relationship has been a private affair, it affects not only their families but all Verona; the lessons it teaches are for all of us.

Characters

The Montague and Capulet Parents

The parents of both Romeo and Juliet play a significant role. As the older members of the opposing families, they represent the feud and the barrier that it places on the lovers. In addition, however sympathetic they are, the parents represent obstacles to the lovers' union simply by not supporting it. Fear of parental opposition is one of the main reasons for the deception that runs throughout the play and which leads to the tragedy.

The Montague and Capulet parents also represent an adult, down-to-earth view of love, which contrasts with the lovers' reckless emotion. Romeo's father, obviously fond of his son, is wary of the boy's depression over Rosaline, seeing it as essentially self-centred (I, i, ll. 147ff). Juliet's parents suggest a marriage partner for her whom she has never met, and try to force this union on her because it is advantageous to her, 'my care hath been to have her matched' (III, v, ll. 178–9), without worrying about love.

Another contrast which illuminates our view of what is happening to Romeo and Juliet is provided by the relationships between their parents. Lord and Lady Montague seem to be close, family people who support each other and have a good relationship. But Juliet's parents show us what can happen when a marriage goes wrong. When Lord Capulet speaks with whimsical bitterness about women marrying early and being thus 'marred' (I, ii, l. 13), we realize that he is referring to his wife. She in turn seems scornful of her much older husband, who, we learn, chased other women (IV, iv, ll. 11–12). We see what can happen to lovers as their marriage progresses, and compare that with Romeo and Juliet's youthful passion.

We encounter the parental characters with various degrees of frequency. Lady Montague appears briefly in Act I, Scene i, trying to stop the fighting and showing concern for her husband and son; she is seen again at Romeo's banishment (III, i); and then we hear that she has died of grief (V, iii, ll. 210–11).

Lord Montague too is seen only in these scenes. Romeo's family life is not as important to the plot as Juliet's, and he himself is not as dependent on his family, but, ironically, the Montagues seem more supportive of their child than the Capulets of theirs. Lord Montague has noticed Romeo's depressed state and is concerned to ease it (I, i, ll. 131ff), and when Romeo kills Tybalt, his father defends him skilfully and effectively (III, i, ll. 184–6). Before his death, Romeo, unlike Juliet, takes care to write his father a final letter.

In contrast, the Capulet parents seem unlikeable, but they are far more complex characters. Lady Capulet is probably still beautiful; it is possible that she is still only twenty-eight years old. But her character is bitter. We have mentioned above the fact that her marriage has been a failure, and suspect, as she urges Juliet to a financially advantageous match, that hers was made for similar reasons. We see that her relationship with her daughter is at best strained and formal, as when she suggests marriage to Juliet (I, iii), and at worst cruelly rejecting: 'Do as thou wilt, for I have done with thee' (III, v, l. 204). She it is who bitterly shrieks for Romeo's death after the fight (III, i) and, when denied, plans to poison him in revenge. Even her mourning for the supposedly dead Juliet seems false – overstressed and hypocritical – for it is she who has been partly responsible for driving the girl to these extremes. Lady Capulet represents one aspect of womanhood – the aristocratic married lady – and it is interesting to speculate whether Juliet, whose determination and hard practicality may well have come from her mother, might have developed as she did, had fate not intervened.

Juliet also shares some of her father's characteristics: his emotionalism and his stubbornness. We first meet him at the brawl in Act I, Scene i, but, like Montague, he also seems eager for peace, as his words to

Paris in Act I, Scene ii, and his curbing of Tybalt at the feast, show clearly.

At first, Capulet seems a loving and understanding father. He clearly dotes on Juliet, 'She's the hopeful lady of my earth' (I, ii, l. 15), and seems unwilling to force her into a loveless marriage like his own. But when Juliet, his heiress, refuses the match he has made for her, his pride is challenged. He falls back on the most vicious parental weapon of all, threatening to throw Juliet out – in those days, it would have meant her ruin – if she does not accept him as her master and his word as law. Whether he honestly believes he is acting for her good or not, his behaviour is horrifying in its violence, and removes any doubts we might have about the wisdom of Juliet's deceiving her parents and convincing them of her death.

And Capulet is deceived – he knows little about people. He knows his daughter so little that she can lie convincingly to him. He curbs Tybalt, but the lad then goes on to challenge Romeo behind Capulet's back. And he keeps his dominance not by good management but by throwing tantrums which cow the household.

Yet, finally, we feel sorry for him. He is as happy as a child at times: at the feast, at the wedding preparations, remembering his wild youth before his wife curbed him. He cannot handle Juliet, and withdraws without getting his own way, only to be delighted and won round when she returns 'penitent'. At her supposed death, though his mourning is self-centred, it is probably genuine (IV, v), and when he learns the true story of the lovers, he is the first to offer the hand of friendship to the Montagues (V, iii).

The lovers' parents are not fully rounded characters; they neither develop nor gain greater insight during the course of the play. However, in the final analysis their place in it is vital because they represent a fixed point from which we see the lovers gradually move away. As they develop and gain insight, both of them, particularly Juliet, become more independent of their parents. Romeo is beginning to acquire self-sufficiency from the start: he will not confide in his parents. Juliet, at first obedient to hers, gradually rebels against what they want and chooses her own path. At the end, she is fully self-sufficient, a married woman, whose allegiance is to her husband, not her father, and who chooses to be with that husband even at the cost of her own life.

The importance of the parents in the play therefore lies in the fact that their influence over their children decreases throughout, and we are thus able to gauge their childrens' development.

Paris

The County Paris is a shadowy character, seen at regular intervals throughout the play, but never clearly defined for us. He is, from Lady Capulet's description at any rate (I, iii, l. 82ff), both handsome and amicable: 'Verona's summer hath not such a flower' (l. 78). He is certainly rich, for otherwise Capulet would not be so eager for the wedding.

His behaviour throughout is impeccable. He is respectful to Lord and Lady Capulet, devout when with the Friar (IV, i) and quietly command-ing with his page (V, iii). His attitude to Juliet is courteous and devoted, and on the only occasion upon which we see them meet, at Friar Laurence's cell, he treats her with affection, just the right amount of possessiveness for one who is betrothed, and yet with consideration.

Does Paris love Juliet? He has not properly met her before their encounter at the Friar's cell, and certainly has not courted her. In today's terms, we would not think it possible he could love her. However, it was he who initiated the marriage proposal, presumably after seeing and admiring Juliet, and it seems unlikely, considering his riches, that he is interested only in her money. Finally, we see genuine grief at her (supposed) death, even to his defending her body against desecration with his life. His final wish is to be buried with her, 'lay me with Juliet' (V, iii, l. 73), and even Romeo recognizes Paris's devotion enough to comply with this.

However, Paris's courteous, formal love seems insipid and insignifi-cant beside Romeo's passion. This is one of the contributions he makes to the play: he provides a parallel devotion for Juliet which highlights the power and vitality of Romeo's love. Whereas Paris's emotion shows no signs of development, Romeo's love matures – as he himself does – to fulfilment.

The form of love that Paris represents – classically romantic, full of carefully considered phrases, planned courtship and bouquets of flowers – is seen to be wanting. Paris does not get Juliet; Romeo – with his impetuous scaling of the orchard wall and equally speedy rush into marriage – does. Of course, it is also true that Romeo dies, but then so does Paris, and there is no doubt whose death affects the audience most.

Paris's final and most vital role in the play, albeit unwitting, is to provide the impetus for the final act of the tragedy. Had his marriage to Juliet not been impending, Juliet would have had no cause to take the potion, and the subsequent events would never have taken place. Paris is a real threat, not because of his actions or because he is a fearful match, but because Juliet wishes to 'live an unstained wife to my sweet love' (IV, i, l. 88).

Though a shadowy figure, then, Paris is essential to the development of the play.

Prince Escalus

Prince Escalus is presented not so much as a character as an embodiment of law and order. We know nothing about him personally, save that Mercutio is his kinsman. Instead, we see, at the beginning, middle and end of the play, a regal figure who dispenses justice to the people of Verona.

Escalus is obviously concerned about the feud; his opening speech shows his real anger at the two families. He takes action, placing the sentence of death on those who fight and talking privately to each of the family heads in turn. When Mercutio is killed, he is once again furious, particularly as it is his kinsman who lies dead; and when the slain lovers are found, he is obviously deeply moved.

Yet, equally obviously, throughout the play Escalus is helpless. This is not because he has no physical power – as he reminds the crowds at the start, he can order them killed. But ultimately Escalus evades his responsibility to keep law and order and does nothing. He states clearly in Act I that anyone caught fighting will die, yet he reneges on this to pardon Romeo and commutes the sentence to banishment (Friar Laurence later hints that even this sentence can be softened and Romeo be brought back to Verona). For all the threatened executions, fines and regal language, Prince Escalus does not keep his word; his justice is meaningless and 'Mercy but murders, pardoning those that kill' (III, i, l. 197).

By the end of the play, he realizes this: 'winking at your discords' (V, iii, l. 294) has resulted in tragedy. By allowing the feuds to continue, Escalus has contributed to the deaths not only of Tybalt and Mercutio, but also of Romeo and Juliet. His sentence of banishment affects the action of the play by parting the lovers, with all its attendant consequences.

It is significant that Escalus appears, like the gathering of families, at regular intervals throughout the play. Law, justice and the ordered world of those outside the family feud begin the play, then intervene at the point where the lovers' happiness begins its downward movement, and appear at the end in order to investigate what has happened and draw conclusions. Escalus cannot affect the outcome, but he offers the shocked and sorrowing comment of the outside world on the tragic events of the play.

Yet, in the end, he too admits responsibility – even more than the parents do – and declares himself (by his kinsman's death) to be punished. His are the last words of the play, and they are intended to represent the world's verdict on the affair.

Benvolio

Benvolio is Romeo's cousin and friend. We first meet him in the Montague–Capulet brawl in Act I, Scene i, where he is trying to stop the fight. In fact, Benvolio plays the peacemaker throughout, representing one attitude to the feud and its conflict: he appeals to the combatants to put up their swords (I, i), tells Mercutio to be silent when he is baiting Romeo (II, ii) and tries to persuade Tybalt and Mercutio to argue 'coldly' instead of fighting.

In all, Benvolio seems a pleasant and friendly lad. He helpfully offers to talk to Romeo about his depression and in fact does cheer Romeo up. He is in good spirits on his way to the Capulet feast. He seems both liked and trusted by Lord and Lady Montague, and, after the killing of Tybalt, hurries Romeo away, thus saving his life.

If Benvolio has a weakness, it may be an understandable bias towards the Montagues, which leads him to alter the truth. His account of how Mercutio's and Tybalt's deaths occurred is not quite accurate: he favours Romeo in his explanation, omits the fact that Mercutio provoked and drew on Tybalt, and relies on the Prince's natural feeling for his kinsman to make him sympathetic.

What role does Benvolio have in the play? Firstly, he is a friend to Romeo. He helps Romeo during his infatuation with Rosaline, and supports Romeo after the killing. He is also a foil to the hero: his light, undeveloped character contrasts with the increasing depth of Romeo's emotions. An essentially peaceable person, he also contrasts with Tybalt, the fighter, who is Juliet's cousin as Benvolio is Romeo's.

In particular, Benvolio's view of love contrasts with Romeo's. Romeo moves from one deep devotion to an even deeper one. Benvolio, seeing Romeo's infatuation with Rosaline for what it is, advocates a more light-hearted, playful approach, favouring many young ladies at once:

> *By giving liberty unto thine eyes.*
> *Examine other beauties.*   (I, i, ll. 227–8)

This view of love is just one of the many that contribute to the overall examination of love in the play. And it is this view of love which in fact initiates the lovers' meeting. Benvolio's suggestion that Romeo should recover from his infatuation by meeting other women at the Capulet feast achieves its aim: Romeo meets Juliet and the romance begins.

Once he has rescued Romeo from death (III, i), Benvolio disappears from the scene of action. Though this might possibly be a device introduced to free the actor for another part, the absence of Benvolio – together with the death of Mercutio – also contributes to the impression we have as the play proceeds that Romeo is increasingly cut off from his family, and therefore increasingly close to Juliet.

Tybalt

Juliet's cousin, Tybalt, is a far cry from Romeo's cousin, Benvolio. He is a 'fiery' young man, a troublemaker, the direct opposite of Benvolio. He actually loves fighting for its own sake:

> *peace? I hate the word*
> *As I hate hell, all Montagues and thee.* (I, i, ll. 69–70)

He attacks Benvolio in Act I, Scene i, is eager to fight Romeo in the midst of the Capulet feast and, unable to find his man after issuing a challenge, in direct defiance of Capulet's orders, is eager to duel with his friends instead, just for the joy of it – and does so. His hot-headed impetuosity directly causes the fatal battle in Act III, Scene i, and he dies as he lived – violently.

Tybalt does not at first seem to have any good points: he is deceitful, cruel and aggressive. However, he is mourned by the Capulet family, even by Juliet, who does not love hatred for its own sake, and one must admire his sheer reckless bravado. Otherwise, Tybalt is almost a caricature of feuding violence.

This is, in fact, his main role in the play: to represent the feud in living form. Tybalt is the kind of person who keeps the feud alive, who hates mindlessly, defends his family regardless and loves killing for its own sake. No other character so clearly shows us the nature of the feud, why it has happened and what it can do. He erupts on to the stage in Act I and haunts it until the play ends, his violence precipitating the whole tragedy, from his sighting of Romeo with Juliet through his killing of Mercutio to the banishment of Romeo for his murder. Even when Juliet takes the potion, she is driven on by her fantasy of Tybalt, again representing the feud. In the final scene, Romeo addresses Tybalt's corpse and hopes to end the feud by his death:

> *O, what more favour can I do to thee*
> *Than with that hand that cut thy youth in twain*
> *To sunder his that was thine enemy?*　　(V, iii, ll. 98–100)

This, of course, he does.

In addition to representing the family feud, Tybalt also represents the Capulet family, and, as such, his death tests Juliet's loyalty. She firmly proves her love for Romeo by condemning Tybalt:

> *And Tybalt's dead, that would have slain my husband.*
> *All this is comfort.*　　(III, ii, ll. 106–7)

Finally, Tybalt provides a contrast with Romeo. Here we have a lad whose age, position and rearing are similar to Romeo's, but whose energies are turned not to love, friendship, laughter and dancing, but to defence of his family – 'honor of my kin' (I, v, l. 58) – even if it costs him his life. In the ultimate test, Romeo too kills for honour – but we know that he is wrong, and so does he. Tybalt, by contrast, never gains such insight and dies unrepentant.

The Nurse

In many plays of the time, both the hero and heroine had friends who supported them and in whom they confided. For Juliet, this confidante is her Nurse.

Juliet's nurse is an older, widowed woman, whose child, Susan, died and who became wet-nurse to Juliet. She is a working-class woman, a gossip and a chatterer, not over-intelligent though full of common-sense wisdom; and she dotes on Juliet, who, we guess, is the centre of her world.

It is the Nurse who fed Juliet, weaned her (I, iii, ll. 25–7) and stayed with her throughout childhood when her parents were away. The Nurse's devotion has been repaid: we see from the first that Juliet loves her Nurse, trusts her, as when she sends her to Romeo (II, ii), and relies on her advice and understanding. And for the first part of the play at least, the relationship works well. The Nurse supports Juliet in her affair with Romeo, while at the same time warning Romeo against 'a very gross kind of behaviour' (II, iv, l. 163). She arranges the wedding and brings the cords which allow Romeo entry to Juliet's room. In return, Juliet panders to her need for attention, confides in her and gives her warm affection.

Then things begin to go wrong. The Nurse supports Juliet in her affair with Romeo, but sees it as just that – an affair, not an emotional bond for life. The Nurse assists Juliet in what seems to her a thrilling escapade without realizing the consequences. When Romeo is gone, and a better offer arises, it seems only common sense to take it up: 'I think it best you married with the County' (III, v, l. 218). The Nurse gives Juliet sensible advice, totally misunderstanding the girl's passion. And, in so doing, she shows the difference between them so clearly that Juliet naturally revolts against what has up to now been a pleasing relationship: 'Thou and my bosom henceforth shall be twain' (III, v, l. 241).

The Nurse, however, does not realize this. She sees a repentant girl who needs her help in organizing her trousseau, and who perhaps treats her more like a servant than before; but she accepts this as natural, and is deceived by it. As she fades in Juliet's affections, the Nurse also slips out of prominence in the play, appearing for the last time to discover Juliet's seemingly dead body and mourn it, which she does with verbose and over-emotional, but probably genuine, grief.

The Nurse's role in the play is a vital one. She is the one person, before Romeo, who had Juliet's heart. In her company we see the dependent, youthful Juliet, until experience, love and disillusionment make her self-reliant.

The girl's confidante, the Nurse, forms a parallel to Friar Laurence: when the two meet (III, iii), they work together to save Romeo's life, the Nurse by practical action when she stops Romeo stabbing himself. Like the Friar, the Nurse represents experienced maturity, which considers life and living far more important than a 'dateless bargain to engrossing death' (V, iii, l. 115).

The Nurse's own view of love is another of her contributions to the play. For her, marriage is a sensible action to ensure prosperity and therefore happiness; and if it involves love, then so much the better. She sees love more as a natural, warm, physical response to another person than as the eternal emotion which Juliet feels. For the Nurse, love is about physical passion, about losing her virginity at twelve years old, about her jovial husband, about sexuality, pregnancy, childbirth and feeding – the full course of life and procreation that she knows so well.

Therefore the Nurse's talk of love naturally dwells on these things, contributing not only a more salacious view of love but also one of the few humorous elements in the play. Her first long speech is a bawdy and humorous reminiscence about Juliet's babyhood, and (to our amusement) she keeps on interrupting Lady Capulet's elevated speech with references to sex and childbearing. During the lovers' relationship she constantly provides a background of sexual jokes, in contrast to Juliet's innocent passion. Nor is her interest all for her mistress: when Mercutio teases her outrageously, we do not believe for a moment that her quivering is due to anger, or that she asked Mercutio's name out of anything other than explicit interest!

The Nurse is a complete woman. With her older, down-to-earth, naturally earthy womanhood, she completes the trio of inexperienced, passionate Juliet, and worldly wise, disillusioned Lady Capulet. Like them, she is, in her own way, strong and self-reliant. Like them, she will not accept behaviour – such as that of Lord Capulet in Act III, Scene v – which she disapproves of. Like them, she speaks her mind and heart and 'from my soul too' (III, v, l. 228).

Yet, in the end, the Nurse fails, for she does not understand her young mistress or her attitude to life. So she loses her, as she lost her real daughter, first emotionally and then in reality. And the saddest aspect of the Nurse's character is that she probably never realizes why.

Mercutio

Young, rich and intelligent, Mercutio stands apart from the antagonism between the Capulets and Montagues, being a member of neither family. Nevertheless, he is the first to suffer because of the feud, and is to a great extent responsible for the remainder of the tragedy.

Mercutio is a complex character: his good qualities, of which there are many, are offset by a cynical, depressive streak. Nevertheless, he is a very attractive person. His bright intelligence shows clearly in the quick, parrying word-games he plays with Romeo and Benvolio. His sense of humour, mocking everything around him, even his fatal wound, appeals to us. His defence of Romeo's honour, despite the fact that he himself is not involved in the feud, gains our admiration.

Even Mercutio's less attractive qualities gain our sympathy. It becomes clear in the brilliant yet cynical Queen Mab speech that Mercutio despises a great portion of humanity, and he quite viciously derides Romeo's infatuation with Rosaline in Act II, Scene i. Unlike Benvolio, whom he accuses of hot-headedness, Mercutio himself is all too ready to fight – in his own way, he is as fiery as Tybalt. Nevertheless, we, like Romeo, want to calm him, 'Peace, peace, Mercutio, peace!' (I, iv, l. 95), for here is a man whose cynicism, even about love, makes him ever restless, whose intelligence makes him ever dissatisfied with the ordinary affairs of men, whose crude bawdiness seems sad beside Romeo's all-absorbing passion. In short, here is a man who is essentially unfulfilled, and so we feel sympathy for him. Benvolio's announcement that 'brave Mercutio is dead!' (III, i, l. 116) moves us all.

It is Mercutio's death which also begins the downward path for the lovers, since it causes Romeo to take revenge on Tybalt. It is with total sympathy that we witness this, because the death of Mercutio, brave and mocking even in his last throes, affects us so much. Romeo's action is not morally justifiable, but it is emotionally excusable because of who Mercutio is. It is also because of who he is – Escalus's kinsman, avenged by Romeo – that the Prince commutes Romeo's sentence to banishment, which further affects the course of events.

Mercutio's other main purpose in the play is to act as a foil to Romeo and his attitudes. Mercutio's liveliness shows us Romeo's quiet courtesy and consideration – look at the different ways in which they react to the Nurse. His cynicism highlights Romeo's quite innocent belief in others. His essential love of fighting for its own sake contrasts with Romeo's unwillingness to fight, until he is pushed to the limits of his tolerance.

But the most basic differences can be seen in their attitudes to love. Mercutio sees love as being based on sex; he scoffs at Romeo's infatuation with Rosaline in the crudest terms, and makes obscene jokes to the Nurse; even the Queen Mab speech contains bitter references to sex. In contrast to Romeo's lustful but essentially innocent physical passion, Mercutio's views seem realistic but also world-weary, and we suspect he is disillusioned with love. He presents yet another aspect of it for us to compare to the lovers' passion.

Mercutio dies in Act III, Scene i, but, unlike Tybalt, is not mentioned again. Yet his influence remains – in fact, Mercutio's dying curse, 'A plague o' both your houses!' (III, i, l. 106), is indeed fulfilled.

Friar Laurence

Whereas the Nurse is Juliet's confidante, Friar Laurence supports Romeo. He is a Franciscan Friar, 'a holy man' (V, iii, l. 270) and a representative of the Church. We know he is skilled in the use of herbs and drugs, and he is also educated in the arts of reading and writing. When we first meet him (II, iii), we see a man both wise and full of everyday common sense, kind to Romeo and yet honest enough to curb him when he seemingly does wrong.

In fact, because of this, the Friar is to Romeo a far better friend than the Nurse is to Juliet. From the start he guides him, challenging his quick change of heart from Rosaline to Juliet, 'Is Rosaline . . . so soon forsaken' (II, iii, ll. 62–3), even though he disapproves of the infatuation. He warns Romeo of the dangers of hasty love (II, vi, ll. 9ff), and when the boy threatens suicide because of his banishment, talks him through his depression in a kindly but forceful manner. Friar Laurence does Romeo both the courtesy of accepting him as a person who combines good and bad parts – he does not, for example, rail at him for killing Tybalt – and also the honour of being honest and direct with him when he considers it necessary.

The Friar does try to do his best for Romeo, and later for Juliet. He arranges the marriage because he hopes it will 'turn your households' rancour to pure love' (II, iii, l. 88). He organizes Romeo's night with

Juliet and his flight to Mantua. Then, when Juliet comes to him for help, he devises a subtle plan to carry out her wishes.

Nevertheless, there are points in the play where the Friar's motivation is suspect. His original agreement to the wedding is manipulative: what did he expect to do after the wedding, or if the marriage failed under the strain of secrecy? Then, when Juliet asks for help, he finds himself in deep water, responsible for a situation that is clearly going from bad to worse. It may or may not be significant that the Friar suggests a way out for Juliet after she has reminded him of his part in the affair, thus possibly making him aware of his guilt and powerlessness. Juliet herself wonders if the Friar wants her dead rather than he be

> *dishonoured*
> *Because he married me before . . .*   (IV, iii, ll. 26–7)

Certainly, when the ultimate horror has happened and Romeo is dead, the Friar leaves Juliet through sheer fear of the consequences; we may wonder if, had he stayed, he might have persuaded her to live.

But in the final moments of the play the Friar regains our respect for the very trait we saw in him earlier – his honesty. He admits what has happened, and his part in it. And, unlike so many characters, he learns his lesson. Willing to take his punishment, the Friar is pardoned because of this.

The Friar is a complex character, then, who gains insight throughout the play. His role in it is considerable, as Romeo's friend – as previously mentioned – and as an initiator of action in the case of both Romeo and Juliet. Both of these roles are vital to the plot and to our understanding of the lovers' characters.

Friar Laurence also offers us a mature view of life which contrasts successfully with the lovers' views. It is an older person's outlook, one influenced by his down-to-earth character and his religious background. He continually puts things in perspective, sees the good in everything and is the restraining voice of sense and prudence. Beside him, Romeo's youthful impetuosity seems unrealistic but, at the same time, attractive.

Beside his view of love, too, the lovers' passion seems naive. He it is who, while fully expecting Romeo to have slept with Rosaline, points out to the boy the essential inconsistency of his altered passion. He it is who, minutes before they marry, issues an (accurate) warning on the dangers of hasty love. Like many adults, he is wary of such violent passion, and the only way he can handle it is with the Church's blessing:

> *you shall not stay alone*
> *Till Holy Church incorporate two in one.*   (II, vi, ll. 36–7)

Yet even while we accept the Friar's view as realistic and the lovers' as naive, Friar Laurence's outlook nevertheless seems unappealing, a constant block to Romeo and Juliet's fulfilment. We go along with him far more when he is assisting Juliet in the rash plan of simulated death than when he urges caution. Like the Nurse, the Friar represents the older generation who hold back the young, and so provides a counterpoise to the lovers: he is someone whose wise words we can agree with but still chafe against, as Romeo does.

In the end, of course, the Friar's collusion in the whole matter is one of the main causes of the tragedy. Finally, though pardoned, he is in fact punished, for the lifelong regret he has to suffer is no doubt as great a punishment for him as execution would have been.

Juliet

The heroine of a play can be such for many reasons. In Juliet's case, she deserves the title chiefly because of the way in which her character develops and matures in the course of the play.

When we first meet her in Act I, Scene iii, we see a child, a young Italian girl of thirteen who has – as was the custom – led a cloistered life away from Veronese society, who knows only her family, who is innocent of the world.

She is also very childish, seeming to accept the world-view of those around her without question, even on such important matters as marriage. She is totally obedient to her mother's wishes concerning Paris, innocently promising that she will only fall in love with him as deeply as her mother lets her!

> *But no more deep will I endart mine eye*
> *Than your consent gives strength to make it fly.*

(I, iii, ll. 99–100)

At this point, Juliet is in fact completely inexperienced and uncomprehending in matters of love. She has not even thought of marriage, and her later words to Romeo during the balcony scene suggest that she has only heard of or read of love-affairs.

Like a child too, Juliet has not gained self-reliance. She relies on her mother for security and direction, and she relies on the Nurse for affection and support. The loving terms by which the Nurse addresses her, and the attention Juliet pays to the Nurse, show the close relationship they have. Juliet, unlike Romeo, has no friends, and so the Nurse acts as friend, confidante and mother. It is the Nurse in whom Juliet confides and whom she sends with messages to Romeo. The Nurse cares for Juliet, calling her in during the balcony scene (notice how Juliet obeys); and, in fact, just as Juliet accepted her mother's verdict over Paris, so she accepts the Nurse's judgement of Romeo. It is under the Nurse's orders, 'Hie you to the cell' (II, v, l. 77) that Juliet goes off to be married.

The impression that Juliet is always docile and obedient is a false one, however. Her childishness also shows through in her impatience, particularly when the Nurse is late back from meeting Romeo. Juliet has not yet learned to control her feelings, and she complains irritably, placing the blame – as many young people do – on the age difference: 'Had she affections and warm youthful blood' (II, v, l. 12). When the Nurse does arrive, Juliet moves from impatience to anger before the Nurse will tell her anything, revealing not only her lack of control but also the fact that, still a child, she has no power over the servant and does not yet command her respect.

What happens to Juliet in the course of the play matures her, both in a general sense and, specifically, in regard to love. It is love which changes her, turns her affection outwards to focus on Romeo and leads her to self-reliance.

The process begins when she first meets Romeo. She is obviously attracted to him – we know she has seen him before they meet because she notices that he did not dance. During their first speech, she quickly learns to parry romantic words and to balance modesty with encouragement. Then comes their first kiss. It is, of course, the first time Juliet has been kissed; they kiss again immediately and with eagerness, and it is obvious that Juliet responds. Her womanly passion has begun to be roused.

Practical as ever, Juliet now goes about finding out who it is she has so impetuously kissed. Already she is practising deception, asking the Nurse about *three* men in order to conceal the identity of the one she likes. Hard on the heels of love, however, comes suffering, and Juliet has to face the fact that Romeo is a Montague.

But instead of changing her mind, Juliet finds the strength of character to proceed. During the balcony scene, she moves from considering the feud to the conclusion that it is unimportant. She also abandons all pretence with Romeo, freely admitting that she loves him. She certainly does not wait for her mother's consent, but follows her own feelings. It is her own feelings too that dictate marriage, and so she dictates it to Romeo. It is Juliet who, in her practical way, suggests and arranges the wedding preparations, while Romeo, enchanted, merely agrees.

Maturity does not come instantly and, as shown above, Juliet's childish impatience comes to the fore again when waiting for news. However, it is obvious that she has changed: she is now ready for passion; her 'wanton blood' is roused; and the child who yesterday was prepared for an arranged marriage now takes her fate into her own hands.

The turning-point of the play, Act III, Scene i, is also the turning-point of Juliet's development. We see her waiting for Romeo to come, still impatient for the night, but now with a new self-confidence, eager for the experience of love.

When the Nurse arrives with the tragic news, Juliet's first reaction is a child-like tantrum, railing at Romeo for betraying her expectations. Almost immediately, however, she realizes her mistake, and in eleven lines she talks herself through to an optimistic view of the situation: 'All this is comfort' (III, ii, l. 107). Whereas Romeo needs Friar Laurence to bring him to this point, Juliet reaches it by herself, showing us her development in terms of both love and family. Romeo is now more important to her than family ties. Admittedly, she then despairs over the banishment and needs the Nurse to suggest that she seeks out Romeo – but then, as we have said, maturity does not come instantly.

We next see Juliet after her wedding night. She is deeply in love, has now experienced physical passion and made the subtle transition from being 'in love' to 'loving'. As soon as she realizes it is morning, she is concerned for Romeo, placing her own wishes and needs after his safety and well-being. She is afraid (and correctly so), but she does not beg him to stay.

Juliet's new maturity is tested immediately. She handles superbly the macabre suggestion of her mother that she poisons Romeo, and shows us how her self-reliance has developed by not allowing her mother to suspect the truth, while at the same time protecting Romeo. Then Juliet is faced with the threat of marrying Paris. At first, she still does not have enough power to act: she begs first her mother, then her father, to prevent the marriage. But although she is rejected by both, she still retains the strength of character and presence of mind not to confess all, beg mercy and give in. She still thinks her Nurse will help her.

The Nurse fails her, suggesting a course of action which would betray Juliet's love and run counter to her beliefs. In this one moment, Juliet fully matures. She realizes that she can rely on none but herself and must now make her own decisions. Immediately she withdraws into herself, and subtly the relationship between herself and the Nurse shifts. It is now Juliet who decides she will go to Friar Laurence's cell, now Juliet who orders the Nurse to convey the news to her mother. She has discovered power, including power over herself and, as she says, in the event, even 'the power to die'.

Juliet has now achieved womanhood. She conceals her emotion in a courteous exchange with Paris, and is resolute in her meeting with the Friar. Despite her very real fear, she agrees to take the potion and does so, having lulled her family into a false sense of security. She is now totally separate from them, 'My dismal scene I needs must act alone' (IV, iii, l. 19). and moves towards Romeo, prepared to face possible death rather than betray the love which is now the most important thing in her life.

We finally see Juliet as she wakes, secure in the supposed knowledge that now she is to be with Romeo. But once she discovers the truth, she does not for a moment accept the Friar's compromise of a convent life: she has no central point now but Romeo. She orders the Friar away, and he obeys. Unlike Romeo, Juliet does not indulge in a lengthy speech, but, her decision made, takes death quickly and resolutely.

We see, then, that Juliet has matured, and in many ways. A child of the feud, she is at first concerned at falling in love with a Montague, 'My only love, sprung from my only hate!' (I, v, l. 138); but soon she realizes that individual people are more important than a traditional family conflict. When Tybalt dies, it takes her only a moment to come down firmly on the side of her heart, and thereafter family loyalty is totally secondary to her love for Romeo. Unlike Romeo, Juliet is always practical about the dangers of the feud – warning him in the orchard, protecting him from her mother – but she also grows to realize how irrelevant it is to her.

In love, as we have seen, Juliet changes dramatically, from an innocent, biddable girl who sees marriage as a formality, to a passionate woman who enters a marriage joyfully and then will not betray it. Even her first attraction to Romeo deepens, after their love-making, to an emotion such that she truly considers his welfare and is prepared to die for him.

What we see, by the end of the play, is a strong and mature woman. Juliet has, in the space of a few days, moved through all the steps of womanly development save childbearing, and has emerged self-reliant, powerful, sure of herself and her actions, and capable of making her own judgements, her own decisions about life and death – in all, a true heroine.

Romeo

Romeo, like Juliet, is worthy of study not only because of our interest in the development of his character, but also because he draws together many of the important themes in the play.

We actually hear about Romeo before we see him, and what we hear is both disturbing and encouraging. Lord and Lady Montague and their nephew, Benvolio, are discussing Romeo and commenting on his present depression, during which he has been avoiding people. His father goes so far as to hint at some self-deception here: 'But he . . . Is to himself – I will not say how true!' (I, i, ll. 147–8). But set against this picture of a mournful, self-indulgent youth is the real concern that all three have for him: he is obviously someone who inspires affection.

When Romeo appears, we see a young, handsome, obviously intelligent lad who has thrown himself headlong into unrequited love and is enjoying the self-indulgence. His language has the artificial style of the classic lover, and he refuses to be drawn out of his depression by Benvolio's arguments. We do see hints of the lively, kindly Romeo, however, when he helps the Capulet servant to read the invitations and later calms Mercutio after the Queen Mab speech.

Despite Romeo's conviction to the contrary, going to the Capulet feast achieves its aim: he sees Juliet and promptly forgets his unrequited love, Rosaline. To say that from this point on Romeo, like Juliet, matures would be an exaggeration. However, he does change – his feeling for Juliet, based on fulfilled physical passion which develops into a real tenderness for her, is genuine, unlike his infatuation for Rosaline. Through love he regains his energy, his love of life. His friends comment that he is back to his real, joking, bright self: 'Now thou art sociable, now art thou Romeo' (II, iv, l. 87). He deals effectively with the marriage arrangements. He even, if only briefly, gains perspective of the feud, trying to make peace with Tybalt, trying to reconcile the families. When he has celebrated his wedding night, Romeo finds a new depth of commitment to his love; for although in the joy of his new-found love he wants to live, still he is prepared to stay with Juliet if she 'wills it so' (III, v, l. 24), even if it means risking his life.

All is not solved by love, however, and Romeo still retains many of his old weaknesses. The chief of these is his impulsiveness. Just as he rushed headlong into infatuation with Rosaline, so he does with Juliet, so quickly that his friends don't even know that he has altered the object of his affection. The Friar is rightly critical of this suddenness: 'And art thou changed? . . . there's no strength in men' (II, iii, ll. 79–80). It is Romeo's impulsiveness which drives him to kiss Juliet before they have spoken more than a dozen lines, which makes him risk death by climbing the orchard wall, which spurs him on to an immediate marriage. The Friar warns him to beware of 'too swift' action, but Romeo does not listen. It is impetuosity too, as well as a genuine desire to avenge his friend, which leads Romeo to kill Tybalt. We cannot condemn him for this act – even the Friar does not – for it is the result of severe provocation set against years of feuding. But when Romeo blames fate after the killing he is wrong: it is his impulsive behaviour that is responsible.

After the killing, another aspect of Romeo's weakness shows itself: his tendency towards self-indulgent emotion, first seen in his pining for Rosaline. Whereas Juliet thinks things through and reaches a logical view of the situation, Romeo dwells on the worst until he drives himself to a suicide attempt. The Friar reproves him:

> *Unseemly woman in a seeming man!*
> *And ill-beseeming beast in seeming both!*   (III, iii, 112–13)

The worst aspect of this is, of course, that Romeo's death would kill Juliet too; he has not, as the Friar points out, really considered her, but is, by his suicide, once more being self-indulgent.

When the Friar points out the facts to him, however, Romeo recovers swiftly and turns his mind to Juliet. Once they have made love, he is prepared to go to Mantua, tries to reassure Juliet and calm her fears, and is content to wait until the situation is resolved. But of course it is not: the false news of Juliet's death arrives with Balthasar, and Romeo is faced with the worst extremity of all.

In the final act, we find a much-matured Romeo, now a married man, who combines some of his old weakness with his new-found strength. On hearing the news, his reaction is as impetuous as ever: he immediately resolves to kill himself. It is true, though, that while paralleling the earlier suicide attempt, this one is far less self-centred: Romeo desires to be united with Juliet, not simply to ease his own suffering. Whereas the previous attempt was desperate, dramatic and calculated to fail, this time Romeo really does want to die. He hides his intention from his servant and makes sure of his method of death.

And there are many signs that Romeo has developed. He treats the apothecary well, though he does pressure him into doing what he wants. He gives his servant money and wishes him well. And when he is faced with the challenge of Paris at the grave and is forced to kill him, he feels not jealousy but comradeship with another admirer of Juliet, and places him in the tomb next to her.

Romeo's death speech exposes his character completely. Unlike Juliet, he lingers over the act, fully expressing his love for her. His speech is full of romantic images, which reflect his state of mind. He is emotional, and he gives full rein to the intensity of his feelings. He is impulsive, and his headlong rush to be with Juliet ends by running on the 'dashing rocks thy seasick weary bark!' (V, iii, l. 118). And so he dies.

In Romeo, as in Juliet, the main themes of the play are focused. He, like she, is a child of the family conflict that surrounds them. Perhaps more than she, he is affected by it; yet, certainly at the start, he seems less aware of it.

Appearing after the first fight, Romeo seems unmoved by it, noticing it briefly and then putting it aside. It is obvious from his mother's comment that he has previously been present at brawls – perhaps this is the reason for his lack of concern. During the balcony scene, whereas Juliet is nervously aware of the problems of their different families and that 'if they do see thee, they will murder thee' (II, ii, l. 70), Romeo disregards the danger. After all, his previous love, Rosaline, was a Capulet, so it is a situation he is used to.

But then Romeo is thrust into the very centre of the feud. He arrives in the middle of an argument between Mercutio and Tybalt to find himself suddenly and unaccountably the object of Tybalt's hatred.

Romeo handles it well, unemotionally, and tries with logic and courtesy to overcome years of inborn aggression. Of course, he fails; in fact, his brave act is seen as 'vile submission' and leads directly to the fight which culminates in Mercutio's death.

Romeo is at once aroused. He becomes caught up in the emotions which have fuelled the feud, keeping it ablaze until now – those of revenge, pride, loyalty. He too turns on the Capulet family (including Juliet) and kills Tybalt. The death seems terrible to Romeo, and he immediately repents. But the fact still remains that, if only for a short while, he is part of the feud. The after-effects – banishment, Juliet's apparent death, his own suicide – directly stem from this one occasion when he was sucked into the conflict.

In fact, though, by his actions – and those of Juliet – Romeo does end the fighting, as the Friar hoped when he married them, though not in the same way. The double suicide makes 'poor sacrifices of our enmity' (V, iii, l. 304) and brings the families together.

Another key theme in the play which concerns Romeo is that of fate and chance. Certainly it is Romeo who sees fate as part of his life; Juliet is far more practical and far more easily takes events into her own hands. From the start, in fact, Romeo sees the influence of something outside himself. He has dreams which disturb him – he starts to tell one of them to Mercutio – and he has premonitions. He feels that going to the Capulet feast will result in 'some vile forfeit of untimely death' (I, iv, l. 111). He sees his life as a boat, directed by a pilot who has 'the steerage of my course' (I, iv, l. 112).

Romeo is certainly correct in one respect, that coincidence dogs his life. As we have seen, many events in the play, including the tragic misunderstanding that leads to his death, are caused by chance. The plot is a series of 'if onlys'. He is also correct to beware of premonitions: his own dream in Act I, Scene iv, is proved true, as is Juliet's fear in Act III, Scene v; his dream in Act V, Scene i, is also a warning of disaster. After killing Tybalt, he curses fate: 'O, I am fortune's fool!' (III, i, l. 136). When he hears news of Juliet's supposed death, he defies the fate that he thinks has dogged his footsteps and resolves to make his life (and death) go the way he wants.

But so many of Romeo's actions are totally self-directed. He goes to the Capulet feast by chance, but chooses to fall in love with Juliet. He himself urges on the marriage and clearly states that he will accept even 'love-devouring death' (II, vi, l. 7) if it is the price he has to pay. He clearly chooses 'fire-eyed fury' (III, i, l. 124) when he kills Tybalt, just as he chooses to join Juliet in death.

In Romeo, then, we see a character through whom Shakespeare shows us aspects of the main themes in the play: love, conflict and fate. We see a character who matures and develops, who, while not as strong as his heroine, nevertheless retains our sympathy and our interest.

Commentary

Time

In the story on which Romeo and Juliet is based, the events were spread out over many months. In order to make the plot more dramatic and to reflect the theme of love as a sudden thing which explodes into our lives, Shakespeare telescoped the events into four days. Although when we think about the plot it seems unlikely that everything should happen so quickly, when we watch the play the speed of events seems totally feasible. This is partly because we are too much caught up in what is happening, and partly because of the intentional inconsistencies in the play which suggest that more time has elapsed between events than has actually done so; for example, the Nurse in Act II, Scene iv, speaks as if she and Juliet often discussed Romeo, and so does Juliet:

> *she hath praised him with above compare*
> *So many thousand times . . .*   (III, v, ll. 239–40)

The actual events of the play occur as follows, all in mid-July, a little over a fortnight before Juliet's birthday on Lammas Eve (31 July).

It is early on Sunday morning when the fight occurs (I, i), after which Romeo enters and talks to Benvolio. In the afternoon, Paris talks to Capulet about marrying Juliet, and Capulet sends out the invitations to the feast, which are intercepted by Romeo (I, ii). Early that evening, Lady Capulet prepares Juliet for Paris's suit (I, iii) and we see Romeo and his friends on the way to the feast (I, iv), which occurs on Sunday evening (I, v).

It is therefore during Sunday to Monday night, after the guests –

among them Romeo's friends – have departed (II, i), that the balcony scene takes place (II, ii). The lovers part when ''tis almost morning' (l. 176), and Romeo rushes straight off to Friar Laurence (II, iii) to arrange the wedding. Juliet meanwhile sends the Nurse to Romeo at nine o'clock; the Nurse meets him (II, iv) and returns to Juliet with news at just after noon (II, v). Juliet goes to the cell straight away to be married (II, vi).

'An hour but married' (II, iii, l. 67), Romeo goes to find his friends, is involved in the fights, kills Tybalt and is banished (III, i). A 'three-hours wife' (III, ii, l. 99), Juliet hears the news (III, ii) and sends the Nurse to Romeo (III, iii). Later that night, Capulet arranges for Paris to marry Juliet (III, iv) while at the same time she and Romeo are celebrating their union (III, v). Romeo leaves at dawn on Tuesday morning, and directly afterwards Juliet's parents tell her about the arranged marriage (III, v).

Juliet goes to Friar Laurence for help (IV, i), returns to beg her father's forgiveness (IV, ii) and, because the wedding with Paris has been brought forward from Thursday to Wednesday, drinks the potion on Tuesday night (IV, iii). She is discovered when Paris comes to wake her for the wedding on Wednesday morning (IV, iv), and is buried the same day.

Romeo's servant immediately rides to Mantua and tells him the news; Romeo buys the poison and sets off for Verona overnight (V, i). In the meantime, Friar Laurence learns that the letters have not reached Romeo, and so he goes to the tomb (V, ii). Romeo arrives at Juliet's tomb at night, late on Wednesday, early on Thursday; Paris and the lovers die the same night; the final reconciliation between the two families takes place on Thursday morning (V, iii).

Notice that there is an error in Shakespeare's timing. Friar Laurence tells Juliet that the potion will make her sleep for 'two-and-forty hours' (IV, i, l. 105). As she drinks it on Tuesday night, she should not wake until Thursday afternoon; but she wakes on Wednesday/Thursday morning.

The time-scale of the play is therefore effectively handled to create an urgent, dramatic story which sustains our interest throughout without seeming implausible.

Love

Romeo and Juliet is one of the most famous love-stories in the world. What many people do not realize, however, is that it is a story about many kinds of love, not just the love between the two main characters. By presenting other forms and other views of love, Shakespeare not only makes the play a far more complex and interesting work, but also highlights, by contrast and comparison, the main love-story of Romeo and Juliet.

The first kind of love that any of us receive in life is love from our families – mothers, fathers, relations. In *Romeo and Juliet*, this love is indeed presented, but in almost all respects it is shown to be sadly lacking. Though Juliet's father calls her 'the hopeful lady of my earth' (I, ii, l. 15), his love for her shows itself only in arranging an advantageous marriage for her, his heiress. When she rejects it, he turns on her with a violence that is frightening; he does not listen to her needs as she expresses them, but is intent on what he has decided for her. Juliet's mother is unable to speak to her daughter on any topic involving depth or emotion (I, iii), and in the same way rejects her when Juliet does not conform to her will:

> *Talk not to me, for I'll not speak a word.*
> *Do as thou wilt, for I have done with thee.*   (III, v, ll. 203–4)

Juliet's Nurse is the nearest thing she has to a mother. We see the affection between them in the way that Juliet relies on the Nurse, who teases and pets her. In the ultimate analysis, however, the Nurse neither understands the girl nor has her best interests at heart: she goes along with the game of marrying Romeo, then neglects Juliet's true feelings at the last minute. The height of insincere love comes after Juliet has taken the potion: her family, apparently deep in mourning for her, are reminded by the Friar that:

> *you love your child so ill*
> *That you run mad, seeing that she is well.*   (IV, v, ll. 75–6)

Of course, not all family love is lacking; for instance, Romeo's parents are deeply concerned over his depression and wish to help (I, i). But we also see that it is family 'love', loyalty and all its ramifications that have fuelled the feud. The family feeling in Act I, Scene i, and Act III, Scene i, and Tybalt's stalwart backing of the Capulet clan actually create conflict. Perhaps family 'love' is not such a good thing after all.

Certainly, we see that in order to progress to any other kind of love, young people need to detach themselves from their families. Romeo has already begun to do this at the start of the play, in his infatuation for Rosaline, which he will not confide to his father (I, i). Both Romeo and Juliet gain independence from their families (and more or less dissociate themselves from the feud) in order to marry, and this independence is finally stressed when they choose to commit suicide for each other's sake, irrespective of their families' feelings. It is ironic that the families' reaction to the double death is their most genuine expression of love for their children throughout the play (V, iii).

Young people, then, as they mature, move from family love to other forms of the emotion. Perhaps the first to consider is what is often described as 'romantic love'. A typical example which might be encountered in the classics would be where a young man sees and falls in love with a beautiful, often unattainable girl, woos her with high-flown language and images, sets her on a pedestal and worships her. There are two examples of this kind of lover in the play: Romeo and Paris. When we first meet Romeo, he is in love with Rosaline. We never see the lady, who seems a classically beautiful, pale, dark-eyed girl. Instead, we hear only Romeo's feelings about her (I, i & I, iii) and Mercutio's mockery of these feelings (II, i & II, iv). Romeo is infatuated; he delights in the unrequited love he feels. He worships Rosaline from afar, defends his love for her most unrealistically, revels in the high-flown, emotive language he uses, and rather enjoys the attention this brings. His own father expresses doubts about 'how true' his emotions are, and Mercutio criticizes him for not being himself. And in the end, Romeo's 'devout religion of mine eye' (I, ii, l. 87) *is* proved false: he forgets Rosaline the moment he sees Juliet.

Paris, conversely, does not betray his love: he dies for her. Nevertheless, his is a classically romantic emotion. He shows a proper sense of decorum in the way he proposes the marriage to her father, and he shows a sincere admiration and respect for Juliet when talking of her and on the one brief occasion that he meets her (IV, i). On her death, he mourns her wildly and with many emotional words, and then vows that every night he will 'strew' her 'grave' and weep for her. Nevertheless, there is something essentially unrealistic about Paris's love: it is considered, planned, classically carried out, but, like Romeo's love for Rosaline, there is something lacking in it. Paris has never met Juliet, but he wishes to marry her. He does not know her, but he calls her 'my lady and my wife'. He worships her from afar, mourns her, but we suspect that it is the distance between them that allows the worship. The real Juliet, ruefully criticizing her own good looks (IV, i), is not what Paris wants. But even so, when he defends her tomb against Romeo, Paris gains in stature in our eyes, and his death makes Romeo – and us – respect him and his emotion.

Another love-linked emotion which is shown clearly in the play is sexuality. The lovers' relationship, with its innocent physical attraction developing into a mature and consummated passion, is set against an almost constant background of sexual references. The first scene begins with bawdy jokes, and this atmosphere is continued until the mid-point of the play, when tragedy takes over. The Nurse interrupts Lady Capulet's talk of marriage with similar humour, on the way to and from the feast Mercutio jokes about sex, and the two together have an amazingly bawdy exchange in Act II, Scene iv. At the end of it, the Nurse says she is 'quivering' – and we are sure it is not from anger!

What Shakespeare is telling us is that sexuality is a major part of life, and not just in a passionate relationship such as that of Romeo and Juliet. Sex can be a normal part of growing up: both the Nurse and Lady Capulet lost their virginity before they were fourteen. Sex is for bearing children: 'Women grow by men' (I, iii, l. 96). When the first innocence is lost, it can become a matter for joking, as with the Nurse, or serious and often bitter satire, as with Mercutio.

And sexual love can also be a threat. Juliet's horror at being forced to marry Paris is not only the fear of being separated from Romeo and forced to keep house for the County. It is also the very real repulsion at having to sleep with Paris and bear his children that makes Juliet long to be 'an unstained wife to my sweet love' (IV, i, l. 88).

Marriage, of course, is yet another aspect of the love-bond that we see in the play. Whereas Romeo's and Juliet's marriage combines romantic impetuosity with a genuine desire to be together, there are other reasons for marriage. Paris wishes to marry Juliet for unrealistic reasons. The Friar sees marriage as a way to unite the families. Juliet's parents wish her to marry Paris – and, the Nurse hints at one point, suitors may wish to marry Juliet – for all too realistic reasons, material ones. The match between Juliet and Paris is seen by her parents in the hardest financial terms. Capulet has fretted 'day, night; hour, tide, time; work, play' (III, v, l. 177) to have her married well. He thinks it utter folly for her to refuse, and even the doting Nurse agrees. For in such a world, a safe financial marriage was essentially a woman's only protection. One suspects that Lady Capulet married for the same reasons; and though disillusioned, at least she has not had to 'hang, beg, starve, die in the streets' (III, v, l. 193).

The relationship which combines, in various ways, all the above elements of love is that of Romeo and Juliet themselves. Their first meeting is, for both, a turning-point. They fall instantly in love and progress quickly through the stages of courtship to marriage and the consummation of their sexual feelings for each other. Their love deepens to the point where – when tragedy strikes – it is for love alone that they die.

Their relationship does have romantic elements. Although Romeo instantly forgets his infatuation for Rosaline, he views Juliet in a similarly romantic light, particularly at first, as a 'saint' whom he dare not approach. His responses to her during the balcony scene use many classically romantic images: for example, 'With love's light wings did I o'erperch these walls' (II, ii, l. 66). He feels violent emotions which override everything else, even thoughts of the future (II, vi).

However, Romeo's feelings for Juliet have far more depth than those he harboured for Rosaline. He reacts to Juliet, responds to her with tenderness, as a real – not an unattainable – person. He becomes himself again – even his friends notice – when he loves her, not a self-indulgent fop. He even gains the strength, though temporarily, to try to make peace with Tybalt.

And Juliet is far too practical to allow the relationship to become merely romantic. She immediately admits to Romeo that she loves him, 'farewell compliment' (II, ii, l. 89), rather than keep him waiting in true romantic tradition. She does not want him to swear his love, but to act instead – consummating their relationship is more important than words.

And indeed we see that there is a large sexual element in the relationship. It is not the disillusioned sex of Mercutio, or the easy, day-to-day bawdiness of the Nurse. Romeo and Juliet move together with awe and excitement, kissing once, then twice, almost as soon as they have met. Their love kindles their sexuality; the Nurse comments on Juliet's 'wanton' blush, and the girl's speech in Act III, Scene ii, is the joyful exclamation of a woman longing to make love for the first time. Romeo too has hitherto been innocent, and his eagerness is rewarded. It is significant that the lovers do consummate their marriage during the course of the play and, by so doing, by becoming sexual adults, bind themselves so closely together that they must be united, even if that entails dying.

Of course, Romeo and Juliet could have slept together without marrying; but they did not. For them, unlike others in the play, marriage is the outcome of their passion. Admittedly, we get the impression that the impetus for this comes from Juliet. She sees no other way to be fully united with Romeo than by marrying him (and in the days where, for such as her, the alternative would have been ruin, she may well be correct). Note that it is she who proposes, not Romeo; but he willingly agrees.

The marriage symbolizes their love; they really wish to be together for life. Whereas the Nurse sees the affair as a simple game in which Paris can be substituted for Romeo when convenient, for Juliet it is no such thing. She is married to Romeo; she cannot remarry and therefore she has to take the potion, and ultimately kill herself, to go through with this.

As well as the three elements we have spoken of, Romeo's and Juliet's relationship adds an extra, vital, factor to our view of love, one found nowhere else in the play. In its truest form, love is a maturing force, wanting the good of the other person, as Friar Laurence reminds the Capulets after Juliet's supposed death. And indeed, in varying degrees, both the lovers transcend their own self-centredness and truly love each other, gaining maturity as they do so.

We can see this in Romeo's behaviour. His self-indulgent passion for Rosaline is superseded by his love for Juliet. For her sake, he honestly tries to reconcile the families when speaking to Tybalt. He is then distraught at the realization of what his killing Tybalt has done to Juliet. After their wedding night, he is willing to stay, risking death, if she wants it. He comforts her when he leaves. When he hears the news of her supposed death, he maturely and effectively arranges his own suicide, with due regard for his servants, and carries that decision through to its end.

Admittedly, Romeo's love is not as mature and selfless as Juliet's. He lets emotion override his better nature in killing Tybalt, and his reaction is selfish, as Friar Laurence tells him:

> *Wilt thou slay thyself?*
> *And slay thy lady that in thy life lives . . . ?*
>
> (III, iii, ll. 116–17)

But nevertheless, he finds sufficient fulfilment in his love to enable him to sacrifice all for the sake of his union with Juliet.

From the start, Juliet learns to develop her innate practicality and at the same time shows great concern for Romeo. She worries that he may be caught by her family when he comes to her during the balcony scene. As a woman, she in fact risks far more by the secret marriage than Romeo does. When the news of Tybalt's death reaches her, she quickly regains her perspective and her love of Romeo, preferring even her cousin's death to the alternative. She too, after their wedding night, puts her own needs second and encourages Romeo to go when dawn breaks. She then behaves courageously and maturely, daring to take the potion, and ultimately taking her own life to be with Romeo.

What we see in the play, then, is a sensitive study of young love which has its human imperfections but is none the less totally genuine, set against a world in which there are many views of 'love'. The result is a study of the emotion which even today ranks among the greatest.

Conflict

The lovers' tragedy is played out against the background of conflict. Conflict highlights the tenderness and warmth which Romeo and Juliet feel for each other, and, by its very divisive nature, makes the unity which they seek, in love-making and ultimately in death, all the more significant and moving. In addition, the signs of conflict which we see throughout the play – the arguments and fights which regularly mark its passage – all serve to make the play exciting, create action on stage and increase dramatic tension.

Although the main symbol of conflict within the play is the feud, this itself is only an outward sign of inward conflicts which run throughout humanity.

Romeo, for example, begins by suffering from an infatuation which he likens directly to a battle, 'O brawling love, O loving hate' (I, i, l. 176), the result of his opposing feelings of desire for Rosaline and resentment that she will not return his passion. He is caught in a self-centred turmoil.

Escalus too is torn between his desire to keep the peace, which he shows by his harsh words and his threats, and his basic unwillingness to take severe action. His proclamation in Act I is contradicted after the fight in Act III: he cannot bring himself to pronounce the death penalty for Romeo. He has realized his mistake by Act V, and we see that a wiser judge would have avoided the tragedy by avoiding the conflict of his own emotions.

But perhaps the most important form of inner conflict is that which seems to exist in the leading members of both families: a desire to keep the peace in Verona set against a need to defend family honour. We find elements of this in almost all the major male characters. Both Montague and Capulet, peace-loving men in private, leap to the fight when a brawl begins (I, i). It is Mercutio who points out that men combine a wish for peace with a natural aggression (III, i, ll. 5–9), and we see abundant evidence of that later in the scene. In particular, we see Romeo calling Tybalt 'good Capulet' (III, i, l. 70) in an attempt to keep the peace, and then, just a few lines on, his blood roused, killing him; at one moment cursing Juliet for their love, which has 'softened valour's steel' (III, i, l. 115), and at the next, weeping in regret. The conflict between war and peace is indeed·a fundamental trait within men.

This inner conflict then manifests itself in outward, visible forms. The major feud is paralleled throughout the play by other interpersonal conflicts. The chief of these is between age and youth, impetuousness and caution, passion and practicality. Tybalt quarrels with Capulet because the older man will not allow revenge on Romeo, and says that 'this intrusion shall . . . convert to bitterest gall' (I, v, ll. 91–2). Romeo meets opposition from the Friar over his change of affections. Juliet quarrels with the Nurse because she will not give her news of her love. Perhaps the most critical conflict, however, is that between Juliet and her parents in Act III, Scene v, over the marriage with Paris. Lord Capulet will brook no opposition, and meets his daughter's refusal with violence; Lady Capulet simply cuts her off. Juliet withdraws from the conflict and takes her own way out – drinking the potion – and in fact can be seen to win. For all her parents think she has submitted, they are in fact the losers.

It is also this basic element of conflict which caused the 'ancient grudge' (Prologue, l. 3). We never learn of a particular reason for the feud, and this suggests that it has arisen from the natural impulses of man to enter into conflict. The play begins with a violent discussion between two Capulet servants of how they will treat the Montagues, and we realize from this that by now the feud has no meaning – it simply is. And it is continued because of the likes of Tybalt, who indiscriminately 'hate[s] hell, all Montagues, and thee' (I, i, l. 70). Tybalt it is who interprets the presence of the good-hearted Romeo at the feast as a scornful gesture and therefore wants revenge; and when he is stopped, he challenges Romeo to a duel. In fact it is not Romeo whom he hates especially, for before the hero enters in Act III, Scene i, Tybalt is quite content to fight Mercutio or Benvolio instead. No, the fight is the thing.

Fights are what begin, punctuate and end the play: street brawls, dramatic duels and, ultimately, tragic deaths. And though they do add excitement, action and emotion, they also remind us that this is the situation in Verona and that it is against this background that the lovers' relationship occurs.

Both lovers begin their relationship by having to face a conflict of loyalties. They are attracted to each other, but belong to rival families: 'I must love a loathèd enemy' (I, v, l. 141). Both reconcile this conflict of interests by allowing love to dominate and by forgetting, to some extent, their family ties. But they cannot forget the feud, and neither can we. Their first meeting is juxtaposed with Tybalt's outburst, and their second takes place in constant fear – on Juliet's side, at any rate – of revenge: 'If they do see thee, they will murder thee' (II, ii, l. 70). In fact, Romeo seems less aware of the reality of the situation than Juliet: he answers lightly, and is not nearly so worried by the thought of loving a Capulet. While she sighs, 'O, be some other name!' (II, ii, l. 42), he changes from love of one Capulet (Rosaline) to another, and jokes with the Friar about 'feasting with mine enemy' (II, iii, l. 49).

But reality soon strikes. An hour after the marriage, arranged by the Friar to 'turn your households' rancour to pure love' (II, iii, l. 88), Romeo kills Juliet's cousin. The blame is not entirely his, since Tybalt's hatred prompted the fighting, and it is surely not easy to remain calm standing by the body of a slaughtered friend. However, the event shows clearly how the feud works: unreasoning hate takes revenge, which in turn takes revenge itself. Romeo is guilty of murder, whatever the extenuating circumstances, and of letting his family loyalty take precedence over his personal love. The attempt at unity through love has so far failed.

But Juliet does not fall into this trap. After an initial outburst, she places her commitment firmly on the side of her husband and against her family. By this time, Romeo too has realized his mistake, and the lovers turn once more to each other, in love and in self-protection. Now, however, the main threat is not the feud, though we hear echoes of it when Lady Capulet suggests to Juliet that the family avenge themselves on Romeo by poisoning him. Instead, the threat is the match with Paris. Had Juliet been able to confess her marriage to her parents, perhaps the crisis could have been avoided. But the feud makes it impossible. We see her take the potion, we see Romeo go to the tomb, we see the double suicide – all because the marriage, born of true love, cannot be accepted in a society whose day-to-day lives are run within a framework of hate.

How far does conflict create the tragedy? It is certainly true that it prevents the lovers from having the unity they wish – marriage – in the society in which they live. Their only alternative, eventually, is unity in death. It is equally evident that the feud – by creating the circumstances in which Romeo was faced with the choice of killing Tybalt – led to this event. Equally, Romeo was a child of the feud, brought up to believe that his honour depended on taking revenge.

Ultimately, though, the roots of the tragedy lie both in chance – an unfortunate combination of circumstances such as the proposed marriage to Paris – and in choice. Juliet chose to pledge her loyalty to Romeo, against her family, and to act accordingly. Romeo at first did the same. In the end, however, he killed Tybalt, and in so doing brought the conflict into his own life and into Juliet's, and thus set the tragedy on its course.

Fate, Chance and Choice

Why does the tragedy of Romeo and Juliet happen? For any occurrences, there are several possible causes, and Shakespeare offers three main ones for the turn of events in the play. On a simple level, many of the things that happen are the result of pure coincidence – chance taking a hand. But there is also an underlying theme in the play that deeper forces are at work, and that fate is causing the tragedy. As we shall see, however, the characters carry out their actions from their own choice and on their own responsibility. To a large extent, Romeo and Juliet choose to die.

Chance does create many of the unfortunate circumstances which occur throughout the course of the play. It is coincidence that the Capulet servant asks Romeo to read the invitation list and so spurs him on to attend the Capulet feast, where he meets Juliet. It is perhaps chance that places Juliet on the balcony and Romeo below it at the same time. Certainly it is a cruel coincidence that makes Friar John unable to reach Mantua in time to tell Romeo the truth, while Balthasar arrives there easily. And Romeo's suicide just before Juliet wakes, though dramatically successful, is also a tragic coincidence. These slips of timing and circumstance make us hold our breath. The last two, though we foresee them because we know that the play ends in tragedy, make us feel helpless and angry: 'If only . . . ,' we think. Considered in this light, Romeo's suicide is certainly an unfortunate chance event.

He himself, however, thinks otherwise. His reaction to the news, and his attitude throughout the play, is to blame, or at any rate credit, fate itself – the effect of the stars upon human actions. We must remember that in Tudor times a good deal more credibility was given to astrology than nowadays. Shakespeare's original audience might have actually believed that the movement of stars and planets caused things to happen to them, and that if stars were in the wrong position, then ill luck would dog them.

The play is interwoven with such suggestions. Romeo and Juliet are called 'star-crossed' lovers (Prologue, l. 6). A general feeling of foreboding, of events beyond the control of the hero and heroine, is gradually built up from Romeo's apprehension of 'some consequence, yet hanging in the stars' (I, iv, l. 107) through Juliet's sudden rush of fear during the balcony scene to her premonition when they part, 'O God, I have an ill-divining soul!' (III, v, l. 154), and Romeo's dream in Act V, Scene iii. Throughout, we feel the lovers are at the mercy of a force outside themselves.

It is Romeo, however, who feels this most. Juliet's practicality dictates her course of action – proposing marriage, taking the potion, preparing to flee to Mantua. Romeo's romanticism leads him to believe far more readily in the idea that fate is guiding his actions. His premonition of danger is followed by his abandonment to whatever happens to befall him:

> *But He that hath the steerage of my course*
> *Direct my sail!*   (I, iv, ll. 112–13)

At first, luck seems to be on his side: he meets Juliet, she returns his love and they marry. But then, it seems, his luck turns. Romeo's first words after the death of Tybalt are: 'O, I am fortune's fool' (III, i, l. 136). He sees everything conspiring against him to make his life a tragedy. And although the curse seems to have lifted when his punishment is only banishment, he then hears the news of Juliet's death and believes that fate has struck again.

At this point, Romeo appears to take matters into his own hands. His cry, 'Then I defy you, stars!' (V, i, l. 24), is the cry of a man who is going to outwit his ill luck by choosing to be with his beloved, to be happy with her, even though it is in death. The audience already know that this course of action is itself an ill-fated one, but Romeo believes that, by his death, he is freeing himself from ill luck and shaking off 'the yoke of inauspicious stars' (V, iii, l. 111).

But are Romeo and Juliet so ill-fated? Certainly, as we have seen, coincidence plays a large part in their tragedy. But present-day audiences find it hard to believe that the stars cause events. So we must look to the final possibility: do the characters themselves create their own problems?

To a large extent, we see that they do. Coincidence may inform Romeo about the Capulet feast, but he goes of his own free will, despite his premonitions. The abandonment to fate that he speaks of does not last long. He chooses to fall in love with Juliet, and he states clearly that he chooses to marry her, whatever the consequences; 'love-devouring death do what he dare' (II, vi, l. 7).

The death of Tybalt, which Romeo blames on fortune, is nevertheless a direct result of his own action. It is an understandable, courageous deed, but it is his responsibility. He clearly chooses his course of action, 'fire-eyed fury be my conduct now!' (III, i, l. 124), and reneges on his former attempt to make peace. The ensuing banishment and separation from Juliet are his punishment.

Equally, Romeo's suicide is the result of his own action. That he received the wrong news is unfortunate; that he responds with a desire to die and fulfils that desire is his decision. He chooses to 'run on the dashing rocks' (V, iii, ll. 117–18) the bark which he earlier trusted to fate, and so he dies.

And so does Juliet. But she, unlike Romeo, does not see fate as being in control of her. Throughout the play, she takes responsibility for her choices: she falls in love, marries and commits herself to that marriage despite all the difficulties. She chooses to risk death to be with Romeo; and on discovering that he is dead, she quickly and effectively – and without reference to an outside influence – chooses suicide:

> *Then I'll be brief. O happy dagger!*
> *This is thy sheath; there rust, and let me die.*   (V, iii, ll. 169–70)

In conclusion, then, we see that although our view of the influence of the stars is somewhat different from that of the original audience, we are nevertheless offered a complex presentation of causes for the tragedy. The ultimate 'why' is a combination of wrongly placed choices and unhappy coincidences.

The Role of Women

At first sight, it seems that the world in *Romeo and Juliet* is a man's world. Lord Capulet is master in his own house, able to dictate marriage to his daughter. Prince Escalus wields his power over life and death. The men in the play, unlike the women, are free to go about alone or gatecrash parties. And the dramatic fight scenes are, of course, dominated by men.

For all that it may be a man's world, however, the female characters in *Romeo and Juliet* are by far the stronger. If they do not dominate the play physically, they certainly do so emotionally, and, in the final analysis, the male characters are seen by comparison to be ineffectual.

Shakespeare presents us with a view of women by providing three very different models: Lady Capulet, the Nurse and Juliet. They contrast in age, class, outlook and personality. Not only does this fact add to the general interest of the play, but it gives us a further insight into its heroine, Juliet.

Of the three, the Nurse is the oldest. Her life has been full of care; her husband and child are dead; her work is hard. She still finds joy in life, however, flirting with Mercutio and gaining great satisfaction from seeing Juliet thrive. And though Juliet complains that the Nurse does not have 'affections and warm youthful blood' (II, v, l. 12), nevertheless the Nurse is both active and full of the joy of living.

In contrast, Lady Capulet, not yet thirty, seems bitter and disillusioned, and her husband complains that she is 'marred' (I, ii, l. 13) by her early marriage.

Unlike both her mother and the Nurse, Juliet is inexperienced in life, particularly in sexual matters. She has not yet lost her innocence or her enthusiasm. At the start, in fact, she is willingly ruled by the two older women, and only gradually gains her independence.

The women in the play span a range of classes as well as ages. Lady Capulet and Juliet are both rich and titled. They carry their wealth easily; Lady Capulet certainly esteems it, has, we suspect, married for it and tries to urge her daughter to do the same by marrying Paris. Juliet, on the other hand, seems to view her position and her wealth as unimportant compared to love:

> *And all my fortunes at thy foot I'll lay*
> *And follow thee my lord throughout the world.*   (II, ii, ll. 147–8)

The Nurse is a servant, lower class and warily respectful of her betters – Lady Capulet – and later in the play, when the girl assumes maturity, Juliet. The question of money does concern the Nurse: she takes Romeo's gold for her services, comments shrewdly that whoever marries Juliet 'Shall have the chinks' (I, v, l. 117) and advises Juliet to marry Paris because he is well placed. Though of lower class than Lady Capulet, she too has a hard-headed, financial outlook.

Juliet's general outlook on life, however, is an emotional one: she sees Romeo, is attracted to him physically and falls in love. Thereafter, she follows that emotion to its logical conclusion. Whereas Lady Capulet sees money and status as the ruling factors in life, and the Nurse too advises Juliet to be 'happy in this second match', Juliet herself follows her emotions, taking the harder but more idealistic route as opposed to the practical, easier one. For Juliet's personality is very different from that of either her mother or the Nurse. She is gentle, kind, emotional and warm. She follows her heart, not her head, she reacts genuinely to Romeo, stepping outside the feud to do so, and chooses death and happiness rather than a miserable life. Compare this to Lady Capulet's hard-headed, logical character: her failed marriage is characterized by bitchy comments to her husband, and there is such an emotional distance between her and her daughter that she cannot talk about intimate matters without the Nurse present. Compare Juliet's attitude to the feud with Lady Capulet's vicious demand for Romeo's life and her later plans for revengeful murder. Compare Juliet's innocent but committed sexuality to her mother's coldness and to the Nurse's bawdy easiness, which advises Juliet to change one husband for another when it suits. Compare Juliet's genuine mourning for Romeo and her own joyful acceptance of death with the more formalized and superficial grief of her mother and the Nurse at her death, unaware that they were in fact partly responsible for it.

Yet there are some factors which bind the women together. All three are practical – all three, for example, see marriage as the end product of love, and Juliet's demand of Romeo that 'thy purpose [be] marriage' (II, ii, l. 144) echoes her mother's words of the previous act. All three are capable of fierce emotion: the Nurse in her fierce protectiveness of Juliet; her mother's vicious attack on Romeo; Juliet's own deep passion.

Finally, all three women are, in their own ways, strong characters. Lady Capulet has, through sheer force of will, sustained a difficult and loveless marriage, and has dominated her husband. The Nurse has had a hard life, and is a strong enough character to rule Juliet, at any rate up to Act IV, and challenge Lord and Lady Capulet. Juliet herself shows incredible strength of character throughout the play, moving from biddable innocence to joyful sexual experience, gaining independence from her family, taking her fate into her own hands. Her love for Romeo so transcends the concerns of the feud that she risks possible death and shame for him, and finally has the strength to kill herself.

Beside this, the male characters in the play seem pale. The lesser characters are weaker. Lord Capulet, for all his ranting, seems inconsistent and ineffectual. The Prince admits his own weakness at the end of the play. The street fights, though dramatically exciting, seem childish compared with Juliet's serene acceptance of the potion. And even

Romeo, though a classic hero, is not as strong as his heroine. She faces up to the reality of the feud and chooses her love while he is still laughingly ignoring the danger. She commits herself to marriage while he still sighs romantically. Whereas Juliet quickly and effectively moves to an optimistic view of the killing of Tybalt, Romeo wallows in emotion until Friar Laurence chides him. And while Romeo airily dreams of his love in Mantua, Juliet is facing potential death in Verona.

In the end, both lovers gain our respect by their suicides. But, in the final analysis, Juliet is the stronger character and dominates the play.

Death and the Macabre

Romeo and Juliet is in essence a love-story. But it is also a play full of horror, terror, violence, murder, feigned death and suicide. Shakespeare builds on our emotion until by the end of the play we are really affected.

The play is shot through with terror, a background atmosphere of fear which both worries us and contrasts with the joy that the lovers feel in their relationship. Both Romeo and Juliet have premonitions: Romeo's 'mind misgives' (I, iv, l. 106); Juliet has 'an ill-divining soul' (III, v, l. 54). Throughout the play there are references to death, often with ironic implications: Romeo thinks Juliet's beauty is 'for earth too dear!' (I, v, l. 47) and himself defies 'love-devouring death' for her sake (II, vi, l. 7); Juliet's mother wishes the girl were 'married to her grave' (III, v, l. 140). All these references both shock us and make us afraid, even though we know the ultimate outcome. Such reminders, spoken by characters unaware of that outcome, increase our fear because they serve notice that violence is very near.

The world of the lovers is, as we have already observed, a world of conflict; the feud is an outward manifestation of this, and violence the demonstration of the feud. As soon as the play opens, our senses are jarred by a quarrel which leads at once – and senselessly – to a fight, and potentially to killings. The Prince halts the proceedings just in time, but we are warned of what could happen the next time the 'bloody hands' strike (I, i, l. 86). Violence is ever present, whether in Mercutio's

Queen Mab speech with its talk of soldiers, or in Tybalt's outburst at the feast or in his challenge.

And it is all senseless violence: Benvolio comments that the 'mad blood' (III, i, l. 4) is stirring simply because of the hot weather. The feud itself is senseless, and what has no cause cannot be controlled and is therefore far more frightening.

When the violence does erupt (III, i), it is horrifying, although the tension is slightly relieved by Mercutio's black humour. But the worst is yet to come. Up to this point, we have not actually seen death – Mercutio dies off stage. Now, with a burst of anger, and just at the point where love has changed his life for the better, Romeo kills Tybalt before our very eyes.

The two deaths almost come as a shock. Though we know the play is a tragedy, we have up to now been caught up with the lovers' own enthusiasm and their innocent belief that because of their love everything will be all right. But now reality intrudes: in the midst of the jokes, Mercutio dies; in the midst of celebrating his love, Romeo kills. We do not mourn for Tybalt, but we grieve for Romeo and the end of any hope that he will survive.

Shakespeare now gives us – and the lovers – some respite. Romeo attempts suicide, but afterwards he and his love recover a little from what has happened and are allowed to celebrate their wedding night. But even as we witness the development of their love and sexuality, terror is never far away, and minutes after bidding good-bye to Romeo, Juliet has to protect him from a threat of death from her own mother: 'We will have vengeance for it' (III, v, l. 87). She copes superbly, but it brings home to the lovers how close the violence is.

Shortly after this, Juliet is faced with the dreadful prospect of having to marry a man she hates. The violent row between her and her parents serves only to increase the sense of desperation and foreboding, and we believe Juliet when she tells the Friar that she is willing to do anything to resolve her predicament. Both in this scene (IV, i) and in the one in which she takes the potion (IV, iii) we have macabre image piled upon image – of various forms of death, torture and madness – all serving to increase our sense of foreboding. The taking of the potion, and Juliet's fear of its possible consequences, the 'horrible conceit of death and night' (IV, iii, l. 37), are indeed terrifying, and prepare us for the final tragedy in the tomb.

Juliet's family, the Nurse and Paris deeply mourn her supposed death. But this is not a true death, and the grieving is inappropriate – and this is apt, for when people do die in the play, Shakespeare allows us to grieve in our own way; he does not put words into our mouths, but lets the horror of the deaths speak for itself. Thus, the mourning over Juliet seems even more overplayed and false. In contrast, Romeo's reaction to the news of her death is brief and genuine: he plans his own death. We, who know the truth of the matter, are both horrified and helpless. We watch as he coolly purchases the poison and describes its effects: 'the trunk may be discharged of breath' (V, i, l. 63).

We come then to the final scene. We know what is going to happen, but we dread it. First, however, we see Paris's challenge to Romeo and his death. We might think that this killing would detract from the impact of the later suicides, but this is not so; in fact, as death piles upon death, so our horror grows. Even innocent Paris dies – as, we learn later, does Lady Montague (and, in one version of the play, Benvolio too). We see that the world is full of death, and that the lovers cannot escape.

They do escape the horrors of life, though, for they choose death. Alone among the characters, Romeo and Juliet make their own decisions about when to die: 'Thus with a kiss I die' (V, iii, l. 120); 'there rust, and let me die' (V, iii, l. 170). Admittedly, this is not entirely an honourable thing to do, and Romeo's first emotional attempt at suicide is strongly criticized by the Friar as representing the 'unreasonable fury of the beast' (III, iii, l. 111). For Shakespeare's audience, suicide would clearly have been seen as a sin.

But Juliet's later, parallel suggestion that she kill herself rather than be dishonoured is seen as showing that she has strength enough to take the potion. And the final choices of the lovers are obvious acts of love. Romeo and Juliet die because they can no longer bear to live without each other.

Despite the almost constant tone of horror in the play, it is, then, a love-story. The lovers' emotion contrasts at every point with the terror around them, and although they die, this too is a joyful thing. Remember too that it is death which finally brings an end to death and the horror of the feud.

Style

However moving a story, however appealing its characters, the play's effect upon us cannot be truly felt if it is not told in words which themselves affect us. The style – the language, the images, the verse in which *Romeo and Juliet* is told – increase its impact on us. We can only fully understand the play by understanding this.

The language that Shakespeare uses continually reflects what is happening in the play. When servants are speaking, the words are simple and direct, often – as with the Nurse – coarse or bawdy. Prince Escalus uses powerful, regal – almost legal – language, such as 'civil', 'citizens', 'forfeit' (I, i, l. 81ff). The Friar uses many words referring to nature and religion: he talks of flowers, honey, roses and ashes, and swears by Jesus and Mary.

Throughout the play, as we know, several themes become clear. And these too are reflected in the language and images. Love is expressed in many different ways. Romeo sees it as 'the devout religion of mine eye' (I, ii, l. 87), and both he and Juliet develop a religious image for their emotion when they first meet (I, v, ll. 93–107). Juliet speaks of love as riches, 'I cannot sum up sum of half my wealth' (II, vi, l. 34), and Romeo uses images of royalty, 'I . . . was an emperor' (V, i, l. 9).

There are also many images referring to the stars, planets, sky, light and air. These often convey emotions of love: Juliet's hymn to the night, asking it to come so that she may enjoy Romeo (III, ii, l. 1ff); Romeo's speaking of Juliet as the centre of his earth (II, i, l. 2), the sun (II, ii, l. 3) and a light that teaches 'torches to burn bright' (I, v, l. 44). These images also frequently refer to fate; the movements of heavenly planets were supposed to affect human actions. So the lovers are said to be 'star-crossed' (Prologue, l. 6), and Romeo dies shaking off 'the yoke of inauspicious stars' (V, iii, l. 111). Find for yourself more examples of such words and images used in these ways.

Notice how some passages in the play, particularly those spoken by

Romeo (I, i & I, ii) and Paris (IV, i & V, iii) reflect the artificial language of love often used in Shakespeare's day. It is full of standard images linked with love, rather than direct statements of emotion. Certainly when used by Romeo about Rosaline, and by Paris about Juliet, it was meant to suggest shallowness rather than genuine feeling. However, this very complex love imagery is also used by the lovers – Romeo more than Juliet – and should also be recognized as a genuine form of the language of love.

Another feature of Shakespeare's language which may seem strange to us is his use of puns. Nowadays, we use puns as clever but always comic jokes. In *Romeo and Juliet*, the Nurse and Romeo's friends certainly use them in this way – as they use bawdy references – but puns are also used in a serious context. So when Juliet hears of the Nurse's news of death, she speaks six lines crammed full of puns on the word 'ay' (III, ii, ll. 45–50), and Romeo's reaction to his banishment puns on the word 'fly' (III, iii, l. 40). This may seem incongruous to us, but try to keep in mind that such clever word-play was appreciated by Shakespeare's audience, and added to, rather than detracted from, the emotion of the moment.

The poetic forms included in *Romeo and Juliet* do vary considerably. They support the mood of each scene and the characters who are playing it. Prose is mostly used by servants – as at the start of Act I, Scene i, or for comedy – as in the respite between the last two phases of the tragedy in Act IV, Scene v. The Nurse sometimes lapses into prose too, especially when she is speaking discursively, and Mercutio rambles on in prose before the fight in Act III, Scene i.

The greater part of the rest of the play is in blank verse. Rhyme is included to add impetus and movement to speeches, to round off scenes (try finding your own examples of this), or where separate characters speak linked lines, as when Juliet and Paris meet in Act IV, Scene i, and parry words.

Several times during the play, often where part of a speech or scene stands as a section on its own, Shakespeare writes in sonnet or half-sonnet form. The two Chorus speeches are separately spoken, and are both sonnets. Paris's speech at Juliet's grave (V, iii, ll. 12–17) is a half-sonnet. Very importantly, the first time Romeo and Juliet meet, they speak in linked lines forming a sonnet and a half. This perfectly reflects the way they are coming together: the climax of the first sonnet leads on to the climax of their kiss.

As we can see, then, Shakespeare uses all the means at his disposal – words, images, verse – to heighten the effectiveness of the story he is telling. You might like to ask yourself how far you think he succeeds, and how far the style of *Romeo and Juliet* adds to your enjoyment of it as a play.

Discussion Topics and Examination Questions

Your understanding and appreciation of the play will be much increased if you discuss aspects of it with other people. Here are some topics you could consider:

1. What similarities can you find between Romeo's and Juliet's situation in medieval Verona and your situation today?
2. Do you think Romeo and Juliet are really in love? Do you identify with their feelings at all?
3. What do you think of Romeo's and Juliet's families? What things about them make you feel particularly strongly?
4. Do you think that the ending of *Romeo and Juliet* is too tragic? Would you rewrite it if you could?
5. What versions of *Romeo and Juliet* have you seen – what acted versions, what televised versions, what filmed versions? Which do you prefer? Have you ever seen a modern version of the play, and what did you think of it?
6. What difficulties do you have understanding Shakespeare's style? Is there anything you like about it?

The Examination

You may find that the set texts chosen by your teacher for the examination have been selected from a very wide list of suggestions in the examination syllabus. The questions in the examination paper will therefore be applicable to many different books. Here are some questions you could answer by making use of *Romeo and Juliet*:

1. Choose a work which deals with the problems young people have growing up. Explain what these problems are and whether you think the work has anything to offer you as a young person growing up.

2. Choose a play which you have studied and have also seen performed on stage. What extra insights did you gain from the live performance? You do not need to tell the story.

3. With reference to two works you have studied, show how the place of women has changed from long ago to the present day.

4. Consider a work you have studied which has as its hero or heroine a person you admire. Describe his or her role in the work and explain clearly what it is you admire about the character.

5. Choose any play or novel you have studied in which minor characters affect the action of the plot in a significant way. Identify one or two of the characters in the work you have chosen and explain how their role in the plot is important.

6. Is death too hard a subject for young people to be studying? With reference to any work you have studied, explore the ways in which death can be presented in a way in which young people can learn and gain from the work.

Examination Questions on *Romeo and Juliet*

1. Romeo calls himself 'fortune's fool'. Do you agree? Discuss the role that fortune and fate play in *Romeo and Juliet*.

2. With particular reference *either* to the Nurse *or* to Friar Laurence, explain how *Romeo and Juliet* can be seen as a play in which older people influence the lives of younger people, usually for the worse.

3. What various aspects of man/woman relationships do we see in *Romeo and Juliet*?

4. 'Violence and death run through Romeo and Juliet; it begins with a street fight and ends with two slain lovers.' Comment on Shakespeare's use of violence in *Romeo and Juliet*, showing how

it adds to the play, and commenting on any ways in which you think it detracts from it.

5. Choose any of the scenes in which Romeo and Juliet appear together and show how their relationship is described and explored within that scene.

6. Comment on the use of humour in *Romeo and Juliet*, showing how it adds to the effectiveness of the play.

READ MORE IN PENGUIN

In every corner of the world, on every subject under the sun, Penguin represents quality and variety – the very best in publishing today.

For complete information about books available from Penguin – including Puffins, Penguin Classics and Arkana – and how to order them, write to us at the appropriate address below. Please note that for copyright reasons the selection of books varies from country to country.

In the United Kingdom: Please write to *Dept. EP, Penguin Books Ltd, Bath Road, Harmondsworth, West Drayton, Middlesex UB7 0DA*

In the United States: Please write to *Consumer Sales, Penguin Putnam Inc., P.O. Box 12289 Dept. B, Newark, New Jersey 07101-5289.* VISA and MasterCard holders call 1-800-788-6262 to order Penguin titles

In Canada: Please write to *Penguin Books Canada Ltd, 10 Alcorn Avenue, Suite 300, Toronto, Ontario M4V 3B2*

In Australia: Please write to *Penguin Books Australia Ltd, P.O. Box 257, Ringwood, Victoria 3134*

In New Zealand: Please write to *Penguin Books (NZ) Ltd, Private Bag 102902, North Shore Mail Centre, Auckland 10*

In India: Please write to *Penguin Books India Pvt Ltd, 11 Community Centre, Panchsheel Park, New Delhi 110017*

In the Netherlands: Please write to *Penguin Books Netherlands bv, Postbus 3507, NL-1001 AH Amsterdam*

In Germany: Please write to *Penguin Books Deutschland GmbH, Metzlerstrasse 26, 60594 Frankfurt am Main*

In Spain: Please write to *Penguin Books S. A., Bravo Murillo 19, 1° B, 28015 Madrid*

In Italy: Please write to *Penguin Italia s.r.l., Via Benedetto Croce 2, 20094 Corsico, Milano*

In France: Please write to *Penguin France, Le Carré Wilson, 62 rue Benjamin Baillaud, 31500 Toulouse*

In Japan: Please write to *Penguin Books Japan Ltd, Kaneko Building, 2-3-25 Koraku, Bunkyo-Ku, Tokyo 112*

In South Africa: Please write to *Penguin Books South Africa (Pty) Ltd, Private Bag X14, Parkview, 2122 Johannesburg*

PENGUIN AUDIOBOOKS

A Quality of Writing That Speaks for Itself

Penguin Books has always led the field in quality publishing. Now you can listen at leisure to your favourite books, read to you by familiar voices from radio, stage and screen. Penguin Audiobooks are produced to an excellent standard, and abridgements are always faithful to the original texts. From thrillers to classic literature, biography to humour, with a wealth of titles in between, Penguin Audiobooks offer you quality, entertainment and the chance to rediscover the pleasure of listening.

You can order Penguin Audiobooks through Penguin Direct by telephoning (0181) 899 4036. The lines are open 24 hours every day. Ask for Penguin Direct, quoting your credit card details.

A selection of Penguin Audiobooks, published or forthcoming:

Emma by Jane Austen, read by Fiona Shaw

Pride and Prejudice by Jane Austen, read by Joanna David

Beowulf translated by Michael Alexander, read by David Rintoul

Agnes Grey by Anne Brontë, read by Juliet Stevenson

Jane Eyre by Charlotte Brontë, read by Juliet Stevenson

Wuthering Heights by Emily Brontë, read by Juliet Stevenson

The Pilgrim's Progress by John Bunyan, read by David Suchet

The Moonstone by Wilkie Collins, read by Michael Pennington, Terrence Hardiman and Carole Boyd

Nostromo by Joseph Conrad, read by Michael Pennington

Tales from the Thousand and One Nights, read by Souad Faress and Raad Rawi

Robinson Crusoe by Daniel Defoe, read by Tom Baker

David Copperfield by Charles Dickens, read by Nathaniel Parker

Little Dorrit by Charles Dickens, read by Anton Lesser

Barnaby Rudge by Charles Dickens, read by Richard Pasco

The Adventures of Sherlock Holmes volumes 1–3 by Sir Arthur Conan Doyle, read by Douglas Wilmer

PENGUIN AUDIOBOOKS

The Man in the Iron Mask by Alexandre Dumas, read by Simon Ward

Adam Bede by George Eliot, read by Paul Copley

Joseph Andrews by Henry Fielding, read by Sean Barrett

The Great Gatsby by F. Scott Fitzgerald, read by Marcus D'Amico

North and South by Elizabeth Gaskell, read by Diana Quick

The Diary of a Nobody by George Grossmith, read by Terrence Hardiman

Jude the Obscure by Thomas Hardy, read by Samuel West

The Go-Between by L. P. Hartley, read by Tony Britton

Les Misérables by Victor Hugo, read by Nigel Anthony

A Passage to India by E. M. Forster, read by Tim Pigott-Smith

The Odyssey by Homer, read by Alex Jennings

The Portrait of a Lady by Henry James, read by Claire Bloom

On the Road by Jack Kerouac, read by David Carradine

Women in Love by D. H. Lawrence, read by Michael Maloney

Nineteen Eighty-Four by George Orwell, read by Timothy West

Ivanhoe by Sir Walter Scott, read by Ciaran Hinds

Frankenstein by Mary Shelley, read by Richard Pasco

Of Mice and Men by John Steinbeck, read by Gary Sinise

Dracula by Bram Stoker, read by Richard E. Grant

Gulliver's Travels by Jonathan Swift, read by Hugh Laurie

Vanity Fair by William Makepeace Thackeray, read by Robert Hardy

War and Peace by Leo Tolstoy, read by Bill Nighy

Barchester Towers by Anthony Trollope, read by David Timson

Tao Te Ching by Lao Tzu, read by Carole Boyd and John Rowe

Ethan Frome by Edith Wharton, read by Nathan Osgood

The Picture of Dorian Gray by Oscar Wilde, read by John Moffatt

Orlando by Virginia Woolf, read by Tilda Swinton

READ MORE IN PENGUIN

A CHOICE OF CLASSICS

READ MORE IN PENGUIN

A CHOICE OF CLASSICS

Hesiod/Theognis	**Theogony/Works and Days/Elegies**
Hippocrates	**Hippocratic Writings**
Homer	**The Iliad**
	The Odyssey
Horace	**Complete Odes and Epodes**
Horace/Persius	**Satires and Epistles**
Juvenal	**The Sixteen Satires**
Livy	**The Early History of Rome**
	Rome and Italy
	Rome and the Mediterranean
	The War with Hannibal
Lucretius	**On the Nature of the Universe**
Martial	**Epigrams**
	Martial in English
Ovid	**The Erotic Poems**
	Heroides
	Metamorphoses
	The Poems of Exile
Pausanias	**Guide to Greece (in two volumes)**
Petronius/Seneca	**The Satyricon/The Apocolocyntosis**
Pindar	**The Odes**
Plato	**Early Socratic Dialogues**
	Gorgias
	The Last Days of Socrates (Euthyphro/ The Apology/Crito/Phaedo)
	The Laws
	Phaedrus and Letters VII and VIII
	Philebus
	Protagoras/Meno
	The Republic
	The Symposium
	Theaetetus
	Timaeus/Critias
Plautus	**The Pot of Gold and Other Plays**
	The Rope and Other Plays

READ MORE IN PENGUIN

A CHOICE OF CLASSICS

Pliny	**The Letters of the Younger Pliny**
Pliny the Elder	**Natural History**
Plotinus	**The Enneads**
Plutarch	**The Age of Alexander (Nine Greek Lives)**
	Essays
	The Fall of the Roman Republic (Six Lives)
	The Makers of Rome (Nine Lives)
	Plutarch on Sparta
	The Rise and Fall of Athens (Nine Greek Lives)
Polybius	**The Rise of the Roman Empire**
Procopius	**The Secret History**
Propertius	**The Poems**
Quintus Curtius Rufus	**The History of Alexander**
Sallust	**The Jugurthine War/The Conspiracy of Cataline**
Seneca	**Dialogues and Letters**
	Four Tragedies/Octavia
	Letters from a Stoic
	Seneca in English
Sophocles	**Electra/Women of Trachis/Philoctetes/Ajax**
	The Theban Plays
Suetonius	**The Twelve Caesars**
Tacitus	**The Agricola/The Germania**
	The Annals of Imperial Rome
	The Histories
Terence	**The Comedies (The Girl from Andros/The Self-Tormentor/The Eunuch/Phormio/The Mother-in-Law/The Brothers)**
Thucydides	**History of the Peloponnesian War**
Virgil	**The Aeneid**
	The Eclogues
	The Georgics
Xenophon	**Conversations of Socrates**
	Hiero the Tyrant
	A History of My Times
	The Persian Expedition

READ MORE IN PENGUIN

A CHOICE OF CLASSICS

Francis Bacon	**The Essays**
Aphra Behn	**Love-Letters between a Nobleman and His Sister**
	Oroonoko, The Rover and Other Works
George Berkeley	**Principles of Human Knowledge/Three Dialogues between Hylas and Philonous**
James Boswell	**The Life of Samuel Johnson**
Sir Thomas Browne	**The Major Works**
John Bunyan	**Grace Abounding to The Chief of Sinners**
	The Pilgrim's Progress
Edmund Burke	**A Philosophical Enquiry into the Origin of our Ideas of the Sublime and Beautiful**
	Reflections on the Revolution in France
Frances Burney	**Evelina**
Margaret Cavendish	**The Blazing World and Other Writings**
William Cobbett	**Rural Rides**
William Congreve	**Comedies**
Cowley/Waller/Oldham	**Selected Poems**
Thomas de Quincey	**Confessions of an English Opium Eater**
	Recollections of the Lakes
Daniel Defoe	**A Journal of the Plague Year**
	Moll Flanders
	Robinson Crusoe
	Roxana
	A Tour Through the Whole Island of Great Britain
	The True-Born Englishman
John Donne	**Complete English Poems**
	Selected Prose
Henry Fielding	**Amelia**
	Jonathan Wild
	Joseph Andrews
	The Journal of a Voyage to Lisbon
	Tom Jones
George Fox	**The Journal**
John Gay	**The Beggar's Opera**

READ MORE IN PENGUIN

POETRY LIBRARY

Blake	Selected by W. H. Stevenson
Browning	Selected by Daniel Karlin
Burns	Selected by Angus Calder and William Donnelly
Byron	Selected by A. S. B. Glover
Clare	Selected by Geoffrey Summerfield
Coleridge	Selected by Richard Holmes
Donne	Selected by John Hayward
Hardy	Selected by David Wright
Housman	Introduced by John Sparrow
Keats	Selected by John Barnard
Kipling	Selected by Craig Raine
Lawrence	Selected by Keith Sagar
Pope	Selected by Douglas Grant
Shelley	Selected by Isabel Quigly
Tennyson	Selected by W. E. Williams
Wordsworth	Selected by Nicholas Roe
Yeats	Selected by Timothy Webb

READ MORE IN PENGUIN

A SELECTION OF PLAYS

Edward Albee	**Who's Afraid of Virginia Woolf?**
Alan Ayckbourn	**Joking Apart and Other Plays**
James Baldwin	**The Amen Corner**
Bertolt Brecht	**Parables for the Theatre**
Albert Camus	**Caligula and Other Plays**
Anton Chekhov	**Plays (The Cherry Orchard/Three Sisters/ Ivanov/The Seagull/Uncle Vanya)**
Euripides	**Andromache/Electra/Hecabe/Suppliant Women/Trojan Women**
Henrik Ibsen	**A Doll's House/League of Youth/Lady from the Sea**
	Brand
Ben Jonson	**Every Man in his Humour/Sejanus, His Fall/ Volpone/Epicoene**
Thomas Kyd	**The Spanish Tragedie**
Mike Leigh	**Abigail's Party/Goose-Pimples**
Arthur Miller	**The Crucible**
	Death of a Salesman
Jean-Paul Sartre	**In Camera/The Respectable Prostitute/ Lucifer and the Lord**
Peter Shaffer	**Lettice and Lovage/Yonadab**
	The Royal Hunt of the Sun
	Equus
Bernard Shaw	**Plays Pleasant**
	Pygmalion
	John Bull's Other Island
Arnold Wesker	**Plays, Volumes 1-7**
Oscar Wilde	**The Importance of Being Earnest and Other Plays**
Thornton Wilder	**Our Town/The Skin of Our Teeth/The Matchmaker**
Tennessee Williams	**Cat on a Hot Tin Roof/The Milk Train Doesn't Stop Here Anymore/The Night of the Iguana**
August Wilson	**The Piano Lesson/Joe Turner's Come and Gone**

READ MORE IN PENGUIN

THE NEW PENGUIN SHAKESPEARE

All's Well That Ends Well	Barbara Everett
Antony and Cleopatra	Emrys Jones
As You Like It	H. J. Oliver
The Comedy of Errors	Stanley Wells
Coriolanus	G. R. Hibbard
Hamlet	T. J. B. Spencer
Henry IV, Part 1	P. H. Davison
Henry IV, Part 2	P. H. Davison
Henry V	A. R. Humphreys
Henry VI, Parts 1–3	Norman Sanders
(three volumes)	
Henry VIII	A. R. Humphreys
Julius Caesar	Norman Sanders
King John	R. L. Smallwood
King Lear	G. K. Hunter
Love's Labour's Lost	John Kerrigan
Macbeth	G. K. Hunter
Measure for Measure	J. M. Nosworthy
The Merchant of Venice	W. Moelwyn Merchant
The Merry Wives of Windsor	G. R. Hibbard
A Midsummer Night's Dream	Stanley Wells
Much Ado About Nothing	R. A. Foakes
Othello	Kenneth Muir
Pericles	Philip Edwards
Richard II	Stanley Wells
Richard III	E. A. J. Honigmann
Romeo and Juliet	T. J. B. Spencer
The Sonnets and A Lover's Complaint	John Kerrigan
The Taming of the Shrew	G. R. Hibbard
The Tempest	Anne Barton
Timon of Athens	G. R. Hibbard
Troilus and Cressida	R. A. Foakes
Twelfth Night	M. M. Mahood
The Two Gentlemen of Verona	Norman Sanders
The Two Noble Kinsmen	N. W. Bawcutt
The Winter's Tale	Ernest Schanzer